Eric LIDDELL

GOLD MEDAL MISSIONARY

ELLEN CAUGHEY

BARBOUR
PUBLISHING

ISBN 1-59789-115-0

All scripture quotations are taken from the King James Version of the Bible.

Cover illustration © Dick Bobnick
Cover design by Douglas Miller (mhpubarts.com)

Published by Barbour Publishing, Inc., P.O. Box 719, Uhrichsville, OH 44683, www.barbourbooks.com

Our mission is to publish and distribute inspirational products offering exceptional value and biblical encouragement to the masses.

Printed in the United States of America.
5 4 3 2 1

ONE

The runners were lining up in their positions on the cinder track. Although no lines were drawn to show them where to be, these men had been in enough races to give each other the space needed.

At least for the moment.

Eric Liddell of Scotland, age twenty-one, known as "The Flying Scotsman," had received a good position, just one spot to the right of the most inside lane. All runners wanted that coveted inside position, especially during the race. Whoever ran there didn't have to run as far, for one thing. And, of course, if no one were ahead of you, you would likely win the race.

To win this race meant a great deal. The winner

today would earn a place on Great Britain's Olympic team and the chance to race in Paris next summer.

Smoothing back his thinning blond hair, Eric glanced to his right and smiled. He knew by name all the runners here, men from England, Scotland, and Ireland, including the man tying his shoes next to him. J. J. Gillies was one of England's best runners, and the favorite to win this 440-yard race. Earlier that day Eric had won the 100- and 220-yard races. No one expected him to win three races on the same day.

As he did with all the runners in every race, Eric offered his hand to J. J. and shook it. But instead of saying "good luck," Eric said, "Best wishes for the race."

Eric didn't believe in luck. To him, all things happened for a reason.

Reaching in his coat pocket for a small shovel, Eric then returned to his starting place. Carefully, he carved out of the cinder track two small holes, just the size of the toes of his shoes. When the race began, Eric would need these holes to help "launch" himself into the race. Most runners brought their own shovels to races. They had practiced carving just the right-sized holes—not too big and not too small—so they could get their best start.

As the runners began to take off their outer apparel of coats and long pants and throw them on the grass, the race official with his flowing white coat made the long-awaited walk toward the track. Clearing his throat, he proclaimed, "Runners, take your marks!"

Eric felt his heart start to beat faster as he crouched down and placed the toes of his shoes in the holes. He knew that he was a poor starter and that he would have to run as hard as he could to finish in the top three. But he would never have another start quite like this!

Out of the corner of his eye, Eric could see J. J. Gillies. J. J. was looking at that inside lane, bordered by a wooden railing. As the seconds ticked by, J. J.'s eyes became like slits. *J. J. is determined to win,* Eric thought. *Are my legs strong enough to give him a race?*

With the small starting pistol in hand, the official raised his arm into the sky. "On the count of three, gentlemen, and then the gun will sound." Seconds seemed like minutes to the racers until the official spoke again. "One, two, three. . ." *Bang!* The report of the gun shattered the nerve-wrenching stillness.

The runners' arched bodies exploded forward until they straightened, their legs and arms making them go faster and faster.

Fifteen yards into the race, J. J. Gillies made his move—the move he had plotted in his head minutes earlier. But instead of waiting for an opening, J. J. cut right in front of Eric! In a second, Eric felt himself lose his balance and go flying into the wooden railing—and then roll over two times onto the grass. Eric sat up and shook himself, then blinked his eyes. Across the track someone was calling his name and pointing a finger at the track. Then another voice demanded his attention.

"Get up, get up!" yelled two race officials, waving their arms wildly. "You're still in the race!"

Eric couldn't believe it. But he didn't have time to ask why. Scrambling to his feet, he hurdled the railing onto the track. By this time, even the slowest runner was twenty yards ahead of him. *There is no way,* Eric thought, *unless it is God's will.*

And then Eric started running. First, he began swinging his arms so they looked like two very active windmills. Then his fists started punching the air in front of him, as if the air were holding him back. When his legs really started moving, Eric raised his knees high, as if he were leading a marching band. And finally, to make himself go even faster, Eric threw back his head, his chin up, his eyes looking to the sky.

Yard after yard, Eric began to catch the pack of runners. His arms punching him forward even harder, Eric, to the amazement of the crowd, was now in fourth place. But he was still ten yards behind the leader, J. J. Gillies.

Even though Eric was from Scotland and was most loudly cheered by Scots, now everyone started cheering and shouting his name. No one could believe what they were seeing.

"Forty yards to go, Liddell!" one man shouted to Eric as he overtook the third-place runner. Forty yards, two runners to pass. He couldn't feel his arms or his legs. He could barely take a breath. Forty yards seemed like forty kilometers to him. But he would not stop.

Again, he willed his arms to punch harder, his knees to lift higher, his arms to swing faster. As he neared the finish line, Eric threw out his chest and his head back one more time—and passed J. J. Gillies to win the race. Eric Liddell had won the 440-yard race by two whole yards.

Eric had used everything he had to win the race. He fell to the ground, gasping for breath. Someone offered him a swig of brandy, but he shook his head adamantly. Motioning to the one who had offered him refreshment, he whispered, "Perhaps a cup of tea?"

All too soon, the extremely winded Scottish runner found himself surrounded by the crowd. There were race officials, college friends, reporters and photographers from the local newspapers, and even children. He could only nod or smile at their questions. They were asking him about the Olympics, about his training program, about his next race. Did he know Gillies before? What would he say to him when he saw him? Everyone could see that Gillies had pushed him off the track.

The reporters' questions seemed to blend together in a cacophony of nonsense. He had never granted an official interview and set little store by public opinion. And then one young man's voice broke through Eric's reverie.

"Now that you've achieved your greatest desire, how do you feel about competing in the Paris games?"

Eric closed his eyes and a curious expression came over his face. *His greatest desire.* Ever since he'd been a young boy, he'd been consumed with one dream. But how could he explain the lure of China when a gold medal was being dangled before his eyes? How could he explain the peace that filled his heart whenever he thought of his beloved parents, whenever he prayed that their mission might be his?

TWO

Siaochang, China, 1906

"Yellee! Yellee!"

Eric crouched down lower in his hiding spot as he heard the noisy footfalls of platform shoes coming closer. He and his older brother Robbie loved to play games with Gee Nai Nai, their *amah*, and hide-and-seek was one of their favorites. As he heard his Chinese nanny call his name—she could not say "Eric" so she called him "Yellee"—he started to laugh excitedly.

Slowly and deliberately her footfalls neared his hiding place. Eric always wondered what took her so long and why she took such tiny steps. Little did he realize the pain she lived with day after day, the result of her cruelly bound feet. The custom among many Chinese families at that time was to wrap strips of cloth tightly around their daughters' feet so that the girls would grow up with tiny feet. As years passed, such tight bindings around the feet deformed the bones, and many girls and women couldn't take a single step without experiencing great pain. But Gee Nai Nai, not a young woman, never complained, and her happy personality was adored by the Liddell children.

And then the amah's face met his under the table. "There you are, Yellee," the amah said to Eric in the rural dialect, tugging at his Chinese-style quilted coat. Laughing herself, she pulled him out and plopped him on her lap. "Enough games for now. It's time for your lessons with Lordie and Jiernie."

Trying not to smile, Eric imagined that "Lordie" and "Jiernie"—Robbie and their younger sister, Jenny—had picked their own hiding places by now. None of them was eager to be in school.

Tagging along obediently, Eric followed his amah to one of the two schools in the mission compound. The other school was for girls. In China at this time, only boys were given an education. When the Christian missionaries arrived, however, they urged families to allow girls to attend school, too. (Unfortunately, many Chinese girls were forced to seek refuge in the homes of the missionaries. As boys grew up, they helped provide money for their families, but girls couldn't contribute in that way. So some families killed baby girls or left them out in the country to die. Those girls who were allowed to live were often terribly mistreated.)

Surrounded by a high wall made of hardened mud, the compound at Siaochang where Eric and his family lived consisted of four large brick houses, the schools, a hospital, and a chapel for church services. The village of Siaochang, which included the mission compound, consisted of small houses made of mud, another high mud wall, and a gate.

The gate remained open during the day, but when night came, the gate was closed and locked. There was relative peace in China now, but for years the people of Siaochang and greater China had feared for their lives. The roots of discontent could be traced to the Opium Wars of the nineteenth century, roots that were obsessively cultivated by the Jezebel-like dowager empress, Tz'u-hsi.

The Opium Wars (1839–43, 1856–60) were trade wars that began when China tried to suppress the opium trade by making it illegal for British merchants to bring opium into Chinese ports. For decades, the British had legally traded opium for Chinese goods, but the highly addictive drug was causing serious social and economic problems throughout China. When the opium trade became illegal, British merchants were unhappy because opium had been their major trade item. War broke out, and China ended up making major concessions to Western nations.

With the Treaty of Nanking, signed on October 8, 1843, China was forced to pay a large fine, open five ports to British trade and housing, and cede Hong Kong to Great Britain. But the Treaty of Tientsin, signed in 1858 and ratified in 1860, would have greater implications for Eric's parents: China was forced to admit Christian missionaries and open travel to Westerners, including passage to the hitherto almost-unknown Chinese interior. In a terrible irony, a later agreement restored the legal status of the opium trade.

The Opium Wars left a bitter taste in the mouths of many Chinese, but few hated Westerners as intensely as Tz'u-hsi. After her consort, Emperor Hsien Feng, died in 1861, the empress became the virtual ruler of China because the heir to the throne, T'ung Chih, was only five years old. When he became old enough to rule, he proved a colossal disappointment to his mother. He not only encouraged young people to travel abroad, but he built a university in Peking where Western ideas were taught. When T'ung Chih died in 1875 at the age of nineteen, leaving a pregnant widow, the dowager empress wasted no time grieving. She quickly appointed her sister's son to succeed to the throne. Hardly coincidentally, Kuang Hsu was also a young child—and so, once again, Tz'u-hsi greedily took the reins of power.

Secret societies had long existed in China, but until 1897 none had been supported so enthusiastically, if unofficially, by many of the royal court, including Tz'u-hsi. Although her nephew was now directing the government, Tz'u-hsi had found a cause she could readily endorse: the Righteous and Harmonious Fists, known to Westerners as the Boxers. The Boxers, who got their name because of their ritual, karate-style movements, were determined to rid all foreigners from China. They believed their bodies could stop bullets and even cannonballs and that no foreigner could fight them and win. To them, foreigners were the cause of the rampant social unrest throughout their country as thousands of Chinese workers lost their jobs due to Western industrialization. One of the Boxers' manifestoes proclaimed their ideology in this way:

> *To be converted to Christianity is to disobey heaven, to refuse to worship our gods and Buddha, and to forget our ancestors. If people act in this way, the morality of men and the chastity of women will disappear. To be convinced of this, one has only to look at their eyes, which are completely blue. . . . Our military strategy is simple: Boxing [karate] must be learned so that we can expel the devils effortlessly; the railways must be destroyed, the electric wires severed, the ships demolished. All this will frighten France and demoralize Britain and Russia. . . . Kill the blue-eyed devils.*

By 1898 Tz'u-hsi was once again in control of China. When her nephew, who shared the pro-Western attitudes of his late cousin, attempted to imprison her, she succeeded in placing him under permanent house arrest at the Summer Palace in the Forbidden City. At the same time, she ordered his favorite wife to be thrown down a well to her death.

At age sixty-three, Tz'u-hsi was more determined than ever to rid China of all foreign influences. The time was ripe for the Boxer Rebellion, and the explosion was soon to occur. The time had also come for the Reverend James Liddell and his wife, Mary, to begin their missionary career in China.

Eric, Robbie, and Jenny loved to hear their mother and father tell stories of what China was like when they had first arrived. During the winters at Siaochang, when they spent most of their time indoors, their parents would first read to them from the Bible, and then continue their stories from the night before, stories that usually ended at a very exciting part.

In the very year that the empress Tz'u-hsi began her third period of rule, James Liddell arrived in Shanghai. Shortly after Mary joined him in 1899, the couple traveled to Mongolia, a northern province of China, to set up a mission station there. Mongolia! The name alone brought to mind jagged, forbidding mountain ranges, never-ending deserts, and wild, roaming peoples.

Eric and his brother and sister often wondered what had brought their seemingly shy and unassuming parents to such a wild and dangerous frontier. But that was before their own faith journeys would lead them to make similar kinds of fearless decisions. And that was before they understood the power of the Holy Spirit, a divine force that could not only bring two people together, but also lead them where even their imagination could not venture.

Drymen, Scotland, located on the southeast corner of Loch Lomond, was home to James Dunlop Liddell, who was raised the son of a grocer. Reserved, hard-working, and pleasant, the Liddells were like many other Scottish families of the era. They were also known for their devotion to God, which sometimes led to behavior unusual for most church members of the time. At religious meetings the Liddells sang loudly and uninhibitedly.

Though devout, James had never contemplated missionary service as a career. As a young man, he was employed as a draper's apprentice in Stirling, Scotland, and was content with that calling until one summer holiday and one not-so-chance meeting changed his course. It was during this respite that a Congregational minister named William Blair struck up a conversation with James, and he shared in great depth the work of his church in overseas missions.

James was troubled in the months that followed. He was sure God was leading him into mission work—but where, and how? Certainly a piece of the puzzle was missing, and her name was Mary Reddin.

When they met at the annual Sunday school picnic in Stirling, Mary, a nurse from Glasgow, was visiting friends while convalescing from an illness. Since neither James nor Mary was from the area, they spent the entire afternoon talking and sharing their dreams. In particular, James told Mary of his desire to serve in an overseas mission, a strong yearning of Mary's, as well.

Following that afternoon meeting, James and Mary enjoyed many get-togethers until Mary returned to Glasgow. Then they began an avid exchange of letters. With each succeeding missive came greater intimacy. Finally, James proposed marriage. Would Mary agree not only to be the wife of a minister, but the wife of a missionary in a distant land? Mary did not hesitate in her answer: Yes, she would go to the ends of the earth with James. The year was 1893.

James immediately applied for an ordination course in Glasgow and, following its completion in 1897, then applied to the London Missionary Society for admission into a course offered for those seeking mission appointments. The society, however, informed James that he could not marry until he completed the course *and* one year of hands-on training as a missionary in a foreign country. The society could not afford to pay for a wife's passage until the husband had proved competent at such an overwhelming calling.

The next year, James set sail for Mongolia— alone. To prepare herself for the rigors of mission work, Mary went to the Isle of Lewis, in the Hebrides, to work as a nurse during the summer herring season. She would be kept busy mending the many cuts, gashes, and even worse injuries suffered by fishermen as they plied their trade with razor-sharp knives.

Although James had shown an aptitude for learning languages and had a good command of Chinese after one year, and while he was still sure of his life's work, his letters to Mary of life in Mongolia were hardly promising. Freezing cold, swirling dust, strange, nomadic peoples, a mission post that was a simple clay building, and mounting political unrest—this was the Mongolia James described.

But Mary Reddin was not deterred. This was the life she had wanted, too, and she would share that adventure with only one man.

On October 23, 1899, Mary and James were married in Shanghai Cathedral. They had no family with them—only their loved ones' blessings and prayers. Immediately following the ceremony, the couple left for the mission post in Mongolia, traveling by steamer to the Gulf of Po Hai and then by train and mule cart to the mission.

Seven months later, the Boxers had them running for their lives.

Indeed, throughout 1899 the terrorist activities of the Boxers had escalated dramatically, with bands of these flailing marauders attacking Christians on sight. Not surprisingly, the peasants in rural China had been most receptive to the Boxers' ideology. These poor people believed that if they did not do as the Boxers ordered, they would lose their crops because no rain would fall. In rural Mongolia, these attacks were repeated again and again.

In May of 1900, a Boxer faction descended on the mission station in Mongolia where James and Mary had been assigned. In the middle of the night, James and Mary, who was six months' pregnant, grabbed one small suitcase and escaped in a rickety old wagon driven by a mule for many miles. When, after several dangerous days, they reached the seacoast, they boarded a boat and sailed once again for Shanghai. In their hasty flight, the Liddells left behind a trunk that contained invaluable information about life on the mission.

Even after James and Mary were ensconced in the mission compound of Shanghai, they could hardly feel at ease. A short time later, the Boxers brought their reign of terror to Shanghai, eventually departing to lay siege to other cities.

But not all Christian missionaries were so fortunate. More than two hundred were killed by the Boxers before the secret group was finally overthrown. On June 13, 1900, after the Boxers had entered the capital city of Peking, relief forces from Britain, France, Japan, Russia, Germany, and the United States attempted to secure their interests in China and protect its citizens. Tz'u-hsi, however, had other ideas. After dispatching imperial forces to turn back these relief armies, she declared that all foreigners residing in Peking would be killed. Finally, on August 14, 1900, the relief forces were able to gain permanent possession of the city, and a peace treaty was signed a year later, in September 1901. China was ordered to pay a stiff penalty over a period of forty years, as well as allow foreign troops to remain in Peking.

And what happened to Tz'u-hsi? The Liddell children delighted in this storybook ending. Disguised as a peasant, the dowager empress escaped from Peking riding in a mule cart, not even recognized by her own guards. Eighteen months after the Boxer Rebellion ended, in a magnanimous move, the British authorities allowed her to return to the Forbidden City. Slyly, she had admitted that she had left the city disguised because she, too, feared the Boxers would kill her. However, under the terms of the treaty, Tz'u-hsi would never again have any real power in China.

On August 27, 1900, while James and Mary were at the Shanghai compound, Mary gave birth to a boy, Robert Victor. When the baby was just a few months old, James decided he should return to Mongolia, despite the Boxer threats that still existed. He had other plans for Mary and Robbie, though. They would go to Tientsin, a city about eighty miles north of Peking and close to the Mongolian border.

But Tientsin had not been quite the haven James imagined. The Boxers had rampaged through Peking, and before they could be stopped completely by the relief forces, their next stop was Tientsin. On June 11, 1900, as Japanese Chancellor Sugiyama stood sentinel at the gateway to the city, he was shot dead by the marauding Boxers, who then terrorized Tientsin. While many women and children managed to escape, those who remained were sequestered with the other foreigners. For two months, the Boxers laid siege on Tientsin before an international military force of eight nations came to its aid.

When the Boxers realized their forces were decidedly outnumbered, they set off boxes of fireworks one night and escaped during the noisy confusion that ensued. They had clearly left their mark on the city. One-third of Tientsin had been burned to the ground.

Throughout the subsequent perilous days, Mary felt she and Robbie were being sheltered by God's hand. But Mary had still received no word from James.

Traveling with Colonel Wei, the commander of a small force of the Chinese Imperial Army, James endured an extremely stressful journey. Despite the overthrow of the Boxers in Peking and the accompanying treaty, reprisal murders in rural villages were common, and the threat of bandits was constant. Furthermore, when they reached the former mission post in Mongolia, the sight was hardly welcoming. The mission had been completely abandoned, and there was nothing for James to do but return to Mary in Tientsin and await a new assignment—and, it turned out, a new member of the family.

Eric Henry Liddell was born on January 16, 1902, in Tientsin. His original name, "Henry Eric Liddell," had been deemed unsatisfactory. On his way to register the birth of his new son, James was stopped in the street by a missionary friend. "What are you going to call the wee chap?" asked the friend.

"Henry Eric," James answered matter-of-factly.

"Oh, my friend, he'll have a hard time at school with those initials!" came the unhesitating reply. Suddenly realizing what the initials for Henry Eric Liddell would spell, James and Mary changed the name immediately—but the story lived on, as a source of laughter and embarrassment to young Eric.

When Eric was several months old and Robbie was almost two, James received his new assignment in Siaochang, a village lying in the Great Plain of northern China, a region known for its extreme temperatures. Siaochang was one of two mission stations in the Great Plain, an area of more than ten million people (mostly farmers) and ten thousand villages. Although the land was considered a drought area and was subject to devastating dust storms, crops did thrive there. In a good year, the muddy rivers caused millet and wheat to flourish as well as soya beans, sweet potatoes, and peanuts.

Again James went first, with Mary arriving in Siaochang in the spring of 1903 with one-year-old Eric and two-year-old Robbie. To reach the mission compound from Tientsin, Mary and her sons had traveled six hours by train to Tehchow, stayed overnight at a flea-ridden inn, and then survived a forty-mile trek by mule cart that had lasted the better part of a day. But Mary's spirits were buoyed at the gate to Siaochang. On a sign above the gate were written Chinese characters which spelled, "Chung Wai, I Chai," meaning, "Chinese and Foreigners, All One Home."

Yes, she believed, *the Boxer Rebellion is indeed over. These people know we mean them no harm.* James, who had been quickly dubbed "Li Mu Shi" by the villagers, a name which meant Pastor Liddell, rushed to sweep her into his arms, and then to hug his precious sons who had survived their earliest years miraculously unscathed.

Eric and Robbie, and later, Jenny, who was born in October 1903, were the only children in Siaochang who weren't Chinese. As they entered school, the Liddell children learned to speak Chinese. Compared to the English alphabet, which has twenty-six letters, the Chinese language, known as *kwan hwa*, has fifty thousand characters or letters. Even to write a simple sentence, Chinese children must learn three thousand characters, or *wen hwa*.

For Eric, going to school with his amah meant learning more and more of these symbols. But Gee Nai Nai was patient, and she loved her time with Yellee, Lordie, and Jiernie, hours spent when Mary made her daily rounds at the mission hospital.

After school, Eric played with his many Chinese friends. He learned how to play Ping-Pong and chess, he learned to use chopsticks to eat, and he learned many Chinese songs. The people of Siaochang were always singing, whether out in the wheat fields, seeding, plowing, and harvesting, or in their mud houses at night.

Summer was a favorite time of year for missionary families on the Great Plain. To escape the intense heat of Siaochang, where temperatures would reach 100 degrees Fahrenheit on most days, the Liddells traveled east to the coast, to the town of Pei-tai-ho on the Gulf of Pei-chili.

Dressed in his one-piece bathing suit held up by shoulder straps, Eric spent his days on the beach splashing and laughing in the warm waters and taking an occasional swimming lesson from Mary. James joined the family in August because that was harvest time in Siaochang, a time spent out in the fields and not in church, and he felt free to leave the mission compound.

In August 1906, James Liddell joined his family at this treasured retreat for what would be their last summer together for many years. After reading his first newspaper at the beach, James made it clear to his family that Scotland was on his mind.

"Mary, you simply won't believe this!" James exclaimed, rubbing his bushy gray mustache.

"Father, may I see, too?" Robbie asked, not wanting to be left out. Eric's blue eyes peered over his brother's shoulder, trying to see what had captured his father's attention.

"Wyndham Halswelle! What a name, what a story for Scotland!"

James was greeted by looks of disbelief. "Whoza-well?" Eric imitated.

Laughing, James explained. "He's the first Scot to win a medal in track at the Olympics, Eric." The boys' faces were blank, but James continued anyway. "Well, Halswelle won the silver medal, or second place, in the 400-meter race."

"Then that means no Scot has ever won first place, right, Father?"

Smiling at Eric's understanding, James nodded. "That's right, son. No Scottish runner has ever won the Olympic gold medal." Thinking a moment, James realized that he didn't want to give Eric the wrong message. "Eric, winning a medal isn't that important. What matters is how you run the race of life. Do you remember what Paul wrote to the church at Corinth?" Reaching on the sand for his ever-present Bible, James flipped the pages to the New Testament. "Ah, here it is: 'Run in such a way to get the prize.' And what prize is that?"

Eric's blue eyes didn't blink. "The prize of heaven, Father."

In the spring of 1907, seven-year-old Robbie, five-year-old Eric, and three-year-old Jenny boarded a German liner with their parents for the six-week journey that would end at Southampton, England. The children were excited at the prospect of such an adventure, but Mary couldn't hide her concern. Eric had been recovering from a bout of dysentery, and the dark circles under his eyes, not to mention his fragile frame, had made her question the timing of this spring furlough.

Just before they left Siaochang, a missionary friend, seeing Eric, had remarked to Mary, "That boy will never be able to run again!" Stroking her son's forehead as the ship trudged along its course, she could almost believe those words. Almost, but not completely.

She had sensed God's hand at every crossroads in her life—at the Sunday school picnic, in the Shanghai Cathedral, in forsaken Mongolia and Tientsin, and most especially in Siaochang, where He had blessed them with years of contentment. Now God was leading them back to Great Britain, to Scotland. He would not forsake His child, Eric Liddell.

THREE

London, England, September, 1909

E ric felt his brother nudge him forward ever so slightly. But his shoes felt nailed to the floor, and his eyes seemed stuck on his shoes! Again, but with greater force, Robbie tried to edge Eric closer to the massive wooden desk that seemed to fill the room. The desk of the headmaster, W. B. Hayward.

As Eric raised his blond head slowly and somehow managed to look straight ahead, he spied a pair of kindly old eyes set in a wrinkled face, a face that reminded him of Grandfather Liddell. After spending a year with his grandparents, the sight of the headmaster pulled at his young heart. At once, Mr. Hayward rose and offered his hand to both boys.

"Welcome to Eltham College! Did you have a good first night here?"

...nd Robbie could have told him that any ...ay from their parents was not a good one. ...their case, the separation was even more poignant because their close family ties had been forged through years of togetherness in the isolated Siaochang compound. During their father's furlough, they had quickly become acclimated to their parents' homeland, drinking in the beauty of Loch Lomond and the soaring greenery that was the antithesis of the yellow dust of China's Great Plain. Being together with their newly acquainted extended family had only broadened their family bonds.

For the past year, the boys had been enrolled in the village school of Drymen. Now, as the time neared for Mary and Jenny to return to China (as the boys' father had left Scotland after exactly one year's furlough), a more permanent situation was needed for the Liddell boys. The solution was typical for the children of missionaries. For the next several years, Eric and Robbie would live at the London Missionary Society boarding school located in the Blackheath section of London, a school whose alumni included the sons of such Christian luminaries as David Livingstone and James Gilmour. Mary and Jenny would share an apartment not far from the school until Mary was sure that her sons had made a satisfactory adjustment.

Hearing the headmaster's question, Eric and

Robbie looked at each other and then at the floor. Their first night at Eltham had been unlike any night they had ever spent—but surely the head-master knew that.

All new students entering the boarding school had to undergo an initiation that the other students had made up. In 1909 the initiation went like this. The older students lined up in two lines, facing each other, with each boy holding a knotted handkerchief. As Eric and Robbie ran between the lines—"running the gauntlet," so to speak—they were swatted at with the handkerchiefs.

They had taken the ragging well, but even so, Eric and Robbie could hardly wait to get back to the room they shared. "It wasn't so bad, was it, Eric?" Robbie had said. But Eric hadn't wanted to talk much. "Is it Mother, then?" At age eight, Robbie, a sandy-haired older version of his brother, always wanted to make Eric feel better.

On his metal bed, six-year-old Eric had tried to curl up into a smaller and smaller ball. He knew it would only be seconds before Robbie would come over to see if he were crying. Sure enough, soon he could hear the padding of his brother's feet crossing the small room. And then he felt his brother's breath against his cheek. "Eric, talk to me. Please."

Slowly, Eric turned to face his brother and his best friend, his dimpled chin quivering. But he said nothing.

29

"You know we will have to get used to this. And we will have to pretend when we see Mother that everything is fine."

Eric swallowed loudly. "Do Mother and Jenny have to go back to China?"

Robbie nodded. "You know they do. That's where Father is."

Closing his eyes, Eric thought he heard Robbie say good night, as he wished with all his might for morning to come.

Now Headmaster Hayward looked the Liddell brothers up and down, from the tops of their sandy-blond heads to the laces on their worn leather shoes. *Robert, or Robbie, as he wants to be called, seems so much healthier than poor little Eric,* he thought to himself. *I must do something about this Eric, yes, I must. No six-year-old should look so pale and so thin! Makes one wonder what life was like in China. . . .*

As if aware of the headmaster's thoughts, Eric and Robbie again gave the floor their most careful attention. But at the sound of the older man clearing his throat, both heads shot up.

"I trust this will be a good first term for you both," Mr. Hayward said. "Besides your usual classes, you'll be learning to play rugby, er, rugger, I think the boys call it. Great sport, rugby! Sure to bring out the apples in your cheeks!"

In the month that followed, "rugger" became a favorite sport of both Robbie and Eric, one that they learned quickly. Although in England rugby (as well as soccer) is sometimes called *football*, the sport is very different from American football. Using an oval-shaped ball—a ball that can be easily bounced and kicked—fifteen-player teams work to score a *try* by moving, kicking, or passing the ball down the field and across a certain line. There is no blocking or tackling in rugby, and no player on a team may run ahead of the ball down the field.

Rugby was such a passion of Headmaster Hayward's that he instituted two rugby seasons per year at Eltham. During each season there would be as many as three or four games a week and many practices in between. And because there are no time-outs in rugby, Eric was becoming stronger and stronger, a fact observed by the old headmaster.

"You must be liking the breakfast porridge, young man," Mr. Hayward greeted Eric one day as he left the rugby field. *The boy's cheeks look as pink as rose petals,* he thought rather proudly.

"Yes, sir," he answered. Eric's blue eyes sparkled and then he laughed loudly. He couldn't help himself because the meals were the same every day at the boarding school, and they were far from appealing. Breakfast consisted of porridge and bread and butter, with jam or marmalade as a special treat. Supper featured a huge hunk of bread smothered in meat drippings. And then there was lunch. . .

"Or maybe it's the meat pudding?" the older

man continued, knowing exactly how most boys felt about that often-served noontime dish. This most dreaded mainstay of Eltham's diet was basically what its name implied—meat drippings on suet pudding.

Eric shook his head wildly, and then ran off as the headmaster shooed him away. *Who would have imagined a few weeks ago,* the headmaster thought, shaking his head. *And it looks as if the boy can run, too!*

As the days slipped away, Mary dreaded having to say good-bye to Eric and Robbie. But after a month in her rented apartment, the time had come for her to rejoin her husband in China. From James's letters, she knew that the situation in China had again become rather tenuous. The empress Tz'u-hsi and her nephew Kuang Hsu had both died in 1908, leaving the door open for new revolutionary forces to gain a foothold. Still, Mary preferred the uncertainty of China to facing the moment when she would last see her ruddy-faced sons.

The occasion of her departure was a rugby game, and as most of the boys' parents were serving as missionaries overseas, Mary would be one of the few in attendance. Because she didn't want her being there to bother Eric and Robbie, she stayed in the headmaster's office until the game began and then went to the playing field.

There were Eric and Robbie, along with the

other rugby forwards, laughing and holding on to each other's shoulders as they tried to kick the ball to the players behind them, signaling the official start of the game. The boys were concentrating so hard that they never saw their mother. Mary smiled and turned away, pleased.

She didn't want to think about the next time she would see Robbie and Eric. She knew it would be years away. *God will take care of them*, she told herself. *God will hear my prayers and the prayers of my sons.*

That night, as Mary and Jenny boarded a steamer ship for China, Eric cried himself to sleep in his little bed. He had waited until Robbie went to sleep; he did not want Robbie to know.

Someday I'll go back, too, Eric promised himself. *Someday Father and I will work together in China.*

Eltham College, or the School for the Sons of Missionaries, as it was also known, was a small school, with less than two hundred students in all. Records from that time indicate that 126 students were the sons of missionaries, fourteen were boarders whose parents weren't missionaries, and forty-six were day students whose parents lived locally. But even so, the boys were outgrowing the gray stone buildings of Blackheath, and headmaster W. B. Hayward went looking for a bigger campus.

In 1912, the facilities of the Royal Naval School,

located in the Mottingham section of London, became available, and Eltham College moved into their buildings. Eric and Rob were excited to find not only more spacious rooms but more playing fields, as well. In addition, the new campus boasted its own library, hospital, science laboratories, and chapel.

Along with the change in address came a permanent change of name: No longer would Eltham be referred to as the School for the Sons of Missionaries but simply as Eltham College.

Eltham seemed like home to Eric and Rob, having lived there now for more than three years. During holidays, often the hardest times for those who couldn't go home, the Liddell boys were either invited to Drymen, Scotland, to be with their father's family, or to the homes of those friends whose parents were not serving abroad. In those three years, while they had not seen their immediate family, their mother wrote to them often, peppering her letters with details of the situation in China.

The China of the empress Tz'u-hsi—one that disdained all things Western—was quickly becoming a thing of the past. A new revolutionary leader had arisen who was determined to overthrow the stranglehold of the Manchu dynasty and bring a Western-style democracy to China. To achieve his goals, which included guaranteeing an income for all Chinese citizens, Sun Yat-sen—a son of poor peasants, a baptized Christian, and a licensed physician—sought the help of the Japanese, who were eager to gain influence in China.

In 1911, Sun's revolutionary forces finally succeeded in overthrowing the Manchu government, and at the beginning of the following year, Sun was elected provisional president of the new Republic of China. (At the same time, the six-year-old emperor, P'u-i, was exiled indefinitely to the palaces in the Forbidden City.) But as had been the case in China's recent history, all was not well in this sprawling country. A powerful warlord named Yuan Shih-k'ai soon forced Sun to step down as president to preserve national unity.

What would this mean to the Liddells and other missionaries? Obviously, the acceptance of Western ideology was a positive, but they feared that was more a veneer that covered Sun's philosophy of Chinese nationalism. Already Sun was gathering support, as well as amassing military strength from Russia, in another attempt to regain the presidency.

While the situation in China was beyond their control, Rob (and sometimes Eric) had plenty of news to write their parents. Their letters brimmed with the enthusiasm of two young men who didn't have to pretend they were happy for their parents' sake—they were! They were also eager to make the acquaintance of a new baby brother, Ernest Blair Liddell, who had been born in late 1912.

Dear Mother and Father, Jenny, and Ernest (someone will read this to you),

First, Eric and I send plenty of hugs and smiles to Ernest, that future Eltham man! We'll be sure to give him his first rugger lesson when we meet him. I mean, a Liddell simply has to carry on the "tradition of excellence"!

So far, so good at the "new" school. Same boys, same teachers (why couldn't that change?), same schoolwork. You will be pleased when you see MY marks for this term (Eric will write you later). Eric is doing all right. Did you know he was in a play? Eric played the dormouse in "Alice in Wonderland" and now everyone is calling him "Mouse"!

But the "Mouse" is not quite like his name. After three years of going through this silly game of knotted handkerchiefs (remember?), your son Eric has finally put a stop to it.

Eric felt sorry for this new boy so he said, "That's enough!" And everyone just stopped doing it. Everyone likes Eric, that's for sure, and I think they think he's different from them (could I tell them stories).

You may not have heard that Headmaster Hayward has retired (how old was he?). Our new head is named Robertson, and he seems okay except for one of his rules. This was so funny, and Eric says it's okay to tell you.

It all started when the head said no one could ride his bicycle in the quadrangle. He said it so many times, we were tired of hearing it. I mean, who would break this rule?

Well, one afternoon when no one was around, guess who comes riding his bicycle in the quad? None other than Headmaster Robertson himself, with his young son on top of the handlebars! I'm sure he thought no one was watching him.

At that moment, your son Eric just happened to be gazing out at nature. When he heard the wheels of the bicycle, he couldn't control himself. So he yells, "Hey, no cycling there!" And then he ducks back inside his room.

I hope you're laughing now! Anyway, the head recognized Eric's voice and sent him to his room without dinner that night, but I don't think he's mad at Eric.

We have been strawberry picking, a first-rate outing, if ever there was one. One of the day students' fathers owns a farm where he grows strawberries—so we help him and help ourselves! This afternoon we are going swimming again and I am excited. As you know, we don't have a pool here at the new Eltham,

so we must travel by train to the Baths at
Ladywell. The boys are already after Eric to do
his funny routine again, including yours truly.

After wrapping a wet towel around
himself, Eric pretends like he's receiving the
"Order of the Bath" from the king. We can't
stop laughing because he looks so silly.

Your last letter said we would see you
soon. We hope so. Eric sends his love, too.

Your son,
Rob

Mary, Jenny, and Ernest arrived again in London in 1914, when Great Britain was on the brink of World War I. After a family reunion in Drymen, Mary went to London, where she rented an apartment for a year. With the war casting a long shadow on the school, Rob and Eric were only too happy to move out of Eltham and live with their family, while still going to school during the day. Many pupils had left Eltham and enlisted in the British army. As the war dragged on, many names were read each morning at the school assembly—those Eltham boys who had made the ultimate sacrifice.

Perhaps the war also played a part in Jenny's decision to attend school in China and not in Great Britain. Although she had enrolled in Walthamstow, a college for the daughters of missionaries, she lasted only a short time. Sensing her unhappiness, Mary brought her back with the family to China where she enrolled in a school in Chefoo, on the Gulf of Po-Hai.

Shortly before Jenny left, Eric shared the results of an exam with her, an exam on which he had fared rather poorly. "I don't think much of the lessons," he said sheepishly, "but I can run!"

Clearly, Eric had discovered athletics as his niche in school, an area where he could excel far more than in the classroom, where he was only an average student. When he wished to sound older and wiser, the fleet young man was especially fond of quoting this motto, recited by the bishop of Pennsylvania at the fourth modern Olympiad held in London in 1908, a motto that appears over the gate at the entrance to the University of Pennsylvania: "In the dust of defeat, as well as in the laurels of victory, there is a glory to be found if one has done his best."

Eric's comments would be all too prophetic once he and his brother found themselves back at Eltham as roommates once again. Although they were well liked at school, they were still each other's best friend—and they were still each other's main competition in sports.

Both boys earned their "flannels" and "colours," or varsity letters, in rugby and cricket, for each of their three final years at Eltham. The intrusion of the war had opened many places on the rugby and cricket teams for younger players, including Eric. In 1916, at age fourteen, Eric's prowess in rugby was already known. Like an offensive end in football, Eric, as three-quarter wing, was known for his speed, and he would streak up and down the outside flanks, waiting for his chance to score.

In rugby and cricket, the brothers played side by side on a team; in track, however, they were each other's opponents.

Rob was a senior in 1918, and he was determined not to let his little brother beat him. In their final races of the year, their closest event was the 100-yard dash, where runners sprint the entire distance to have a chance of winning.

As usual, the brothers shook hands before the race. Eric wanted to win, but at the same time, he wanted Rob to win, too. When the gun sounded, Rob got off to a better start, but Eric soon caught up with him. The other runners had dropped back. The finish line flapped just ahead in the wind.

Throwing his head back and his chest out, Eric crossed the line just ahead of Rob, winning by a step. He had tied the school record, running the event in 10.8 seconds.

Rob, however, was quick to even the score, winning the steeplechase (a combination of hurdles and running), the high jump, and the hurdles. Eric, who later won the 440-yard race and the long jump, was voted Eltham's best overall athlete for

1918. At the unprecedented age of sixteen, Eric was also presented the Blackheath Cup, named for the school's original site, an award given only once to a student. (The year before, Rob had won the coveted award.) This list is the record of the top two finishers in final track events for 1918:

Cross country	1) R. Liddell	2) E. H. Liddell
Long jump	1) E. H. Liddell	2) R. Liddell
High jump	1) R. Liddell	2) E. H. Liddell
100 yards	1) E. H. Liddell	2) R. Liddell
Hurdle race	1) R. Liddell	2) E. H. Liddell
Quarter mile	1) E. H. Liddell	2) R. Liddell

When World War I ended later that year, Rob went on with his plans to attend the medical college of Edinburgh University. There he joined students from all over Great Britain who had come to study at the institution, whose alumni included Dr. Benjamin Rush, Charles Darwin, Joseph Lister and James Syme, and James Y. Simpson.

Not coincidentally, with Rob's absence, Eric emerged as more of a campus leader. He became a school prefect and captain of both the cricket and rugby teams. At a race in 1919, Eric beat his old record for the 100-yard dash, with a time of 10.2 seconds, a record that would not be broken at Eltham for eighty years. Eric also won the 1919 Senior Athletics Championship in track, which Rob had won the year before.

But it was about Eric's behavior away from the playing fields that Headmaster George Robertson had this to say of the determined young man: "Eric was entirely without vanity, yet he was enormously popular. Very early he showed signs of real character. His standards had been set for him long before he came to school. There was no false pride about him, but he knew what he stood for."

Although not required by the school, Eric began attending Eltham's Bible studies regularly, never missing one. He was confirmed in the Scottish Congregational Church, a denomination that maintained a strong relationship with Eltham and the London Missionary Society. While he said very little at these Bible studies, nonetheless, he found himself accepting the truth of the messages. Eric was undoubtedly influenced at this time by his science teacher, A. P. Cullen, with whom he maintained a close relationship. Cullen would leave Eltham the year before Eric's graduation to teach at the Anglo-Chinese College in Tientsin. (Cullen would be the only person to have been with Eric during all three major periods of his life: his early youth, his athletic career, and his missionary service in China.)

As evidence that the love of God was beginning to grow within him, Eric began visiting the sick at the nearby Islington Medical Mission, a pursuit that would hold him in good stead many years later. More important to his Christian walk, perhaps, was his reputation at school, where he was a friend to all boys, but especially to those who were not as physically gifted as he. He would graduate not as Eltham's top student—as his brother Rob had done previously—but as a fair and talented Christian competitor, certainly one of the brightest lights to grace the Eltham playing fields.

In the spring of 1920, Mary, Jenny, and Ernest returned to Scotland. As she and her younger children descended the platform at Waverley Station in Edinburgh, Mary clasped her hand over her mouth. It had been five years since she had seen Rob and Eric, and in that time, her rollicking blond boys had become men. As her two strapping sons threw their arms around her and squeezed her tightly, Mary laughed and cried at the same time. She could only imagine what James would think when he encountered the same sight months later. The last time James had seen them, Rob was eight and Eric only six.

To accommodate their large family, James and Mary rented a house in a quiet neighborhood in Edinburgh—21 Gillespie Crescent—to be near Rob, who still attended the medical college of Edinburgh University, and Eric, who had plans to attend Heriot-Watt College of Edinburgh University in the fall.

That summer Eric passed all of his examinations

but one required for matriculation at the university. The glaring exception was French. To rectify the situation, Eric hired a private tutor in French to help him study at night, and to pay for the tutor, he took a job at a farm outside the city limits. Every morning he would rise at six, grab a bite to eat, and then hop on his bicycle for his ride to the fields, only to return after dusk to hit the books.

But that summer of 1920 was not without certain pleasures, as the Olympics were once again the talk of the Liddell household. The 1916 games had been canceled due to the war, and that had only served to magnify the importance of this latest international competition. The conclusion of World War I had brought both victory parades and the heartbreak of disabled veterans, a careening economy and, perhaps therapeutically, a renewed interest in athletic competition. Many former champions had returned to their homeland ready to trade their guns for relay batons and their marching boots for racing shoes in the interest of Olympic gold.

Mary shook her head as her grown sons read every newspaper article, eager for the race times from Antwerp, Belgium. "Who'll be the next Wyndham Halswelle?" she asked seriously. Sadly, the famed Scottish athlete, a captain in World War I, had not returned from the battlefields, and all Scotland had mourned his passing.

Shrugging his shoulders, Rob pointed to Eric, who seemed to hold the papers higher at the mention of Halswelle's name. It had been months since Eric had participated in track competitions, and those had been at the lowly level of Eltham College. But his siblings would not be deterred.

"Yes, Rob, I think he's sitting right here, too," Jenny chimed in.

FOUR

Edinburgh, Scotland, 1921–23

Olympics or no Olympics, Eric Liddell would not set foot on a track for almost a year. Rather, from September 1920 to April 1921, Eric was to be found riding his bicycle three miles daily from his parents' home to the Heriot-Watt campus of Edinburgh University. A science major, he found the transition from sheltered boarding school to world-class university difficult and the schoolwork intense—not to mention living with his parents for the first time in many years.

The time away from athletic competition caused him to focus on his life's ambition, or rather to define it more concretely. Eric was now determined to follow Eltham faculty member A. P. Cullen to China as a science teacher at the Anglo-Chinese

College in Tientsin. Although he and Rob were regular participants in services at Morningside Congregational Church, just down the street from their home, Eric was unsure whether he wanted to follow his father into the ministry. The question of ordination would be postponed for a few years, he decided.

During the winter of 1921, the Liddells moved to a furnished house at 4 Merchiston Place, a location that proved quite convenient for Eric. Only four blocks away was the famed Craiglockhart Sports Complex, the site of many Edinburgh University athletic events, including the annual University Sports, a track competition.

When a friend who had heard about Eric's glory days at Eltham approached him about entering the May 28 competition, Eric demurred. He was too busy to train, and besides, during the upcoming spring holiday, he and some friends had plans to bike to the top of towering Ben Nevis, a 4,000-foot peak about 125 miles northwest of Edinburgh.

Upon his return from the biking expedition, Eric was so physically wrung out that he realized even biking to class was out of the question! Nevertheless, after his recovery from the grueling cross-country cycling adventure, Eric reconsidered his friend's suggestion and decided to start running again, just for fun.

At the University Sports, in the first heat of the 100-yard dash, even a casual observer might have agreed with the writer for the Edinburgh University undergraduate magazine. "A new luminary of the first magnitude has appeared in the firmament," declared the glorious review of Eric Liddell, and soon all eyes were following the once anonymous student. In that heat, Eric came within inches of beating G. Innes Stewart, the man considered the next Scottish champion; in the final, Eric succeeded, finishing with a time of 10.4 seconds. In the 200-yard race, Stewart edged out Eric by a foot, winning with a time of 23.4 seconds.

Less than a month later, on June 18, Eric had a sensational showing at the Scottish InterVarsity Sports Meet, an event similar to the NCAA competition in the United States. After making it through the qualifying heats with no difficulty, Eric won both the 100-yard and 220-yard sprints, and his time in the latter race of 22.4 seconds was considered outstanding. A few days later, the scene was repeated at the Scottish Amateur Athletics Association Championship, held at Hampden Park in Glasgow. There Eric won both races again; his winning time in the 220-yard race, 22.6 seconds, was a Scottish AAA record.

This "new luminary," whom even G. Innes Stewart dubbed "a new power in Scottish athletics," certainly looked like the genuine article to the powers that be at Edinburgh University. Upon his return to the campus, Eric was granted a privilege reserved for only the best and the brightest: an athletic trainer.

Looking around him, Eric couldn't believe a place like Powderhall Stadium even existed. For one thing, the two-tiered oval-shaped tracks were paved with cinders, not grass or dirt. Taking a deep breath, he took in the empty stadium stands, the deep blue sky, the perfectly shaped coal-black tracks, and the yipping sounds of barking dogs. Powderhall, located halfway between Edinburgh University and the harbor district, was also home to greyhound racing, a popular betting sport in Scotland. The upper track was reserved for two-legged runners, while the lower one was reserved for their canine counterparts. Eric was relieved to discover, however, that the dogs were restricted to training on different days.

But that wasn't all. Eric almost started laughing as he watched several athletes prepare for their training. As soon as they arrived, they took off their long overcoats to reveal what to him were ridiculous looking baggy shorts. Then they began jumping up and down and stretching their arms and legs in all directions. And to think he would have to come here three times a week!

As he looked down at his feet to keep from laughing, Eric saw the shadow of a man approaching. Then he felt a tap on his shoulder.

"Excuse me, but you are Eric Liddell, are you not?"

Straightening, Eric looked up slightly to face an older man. "I am."

"Tom McKerchar," the smiling man said, extending his hand. "I'm an athletics trainer at the university. I was told I'd find you here."

As he shook the sturdy, well-muscled hand of the man he had been told was the finest trainer Edinburgh could provide, Eric knew he must accept the inevitable. He had been given this talent from God, and this man wanted to make sure he used it fully. Still, Eric couldn't quite submit to all this attention without an argument. "I know you're supposed to help, but what more can you tell me than to run as fast as I can?"

Rubbing his chin, Tom McKerchar looked at the ground and then into Eric's bright blue eyes. "Well, young man, let's just say I've seen you race. . . ."

As a witness to all of Eric's university races thus far, Tom McKerchar had never seen anyone run like Eric did. To Tom, Eric looked more like a prancing circus pony than a world-class runner. But McKerchar knew he could work with Eric, and he knew he could help Eric run faster even if he didn't change his unusual "windmill" style. First, though, Eric had to want to work with him.

That night Eric asked his mother what she

thought. Sitting together at the kitchen table, she reached for Eric's strong hand. Eric loved the feel of her hands, hands made strong by work and years spent in the harsh Chinese climate. Hands that had always calmed him and then gently urged him in the right direction. Hands that prayed to God.

"Mother, does God really want me to run?"

Turning his hand several times in her own, the older woman looked at her grown son. "God has given you a tremendous gift, Eric, of that I am sure."

"But you know my plans. You know that I have always wanted to work eventually with Father in China, and first with Professor Cullen. How will my running—and now all this training—help me get there?"

"You won't go to China for a few years, Eric. And how long can you run like this? I believe the answer is the same: a few years. Perhaps this is God's plan. To run now, and to give God all the glory for your gift."

Eric's face broke out in a huge grin, and he nodded his head repeatedly. "You know, when I run, I do feel like I'm running for God. Guess tomorrow they can start laughing at me at Powderhall!"

In Europe at this time, all athletic training was done only within the confines of a stadium—never in public. It was considered shocking to exercise outside in a park or on the street, especially in shorts. So three times a week, Eric met Tom McKerchar at Powderhall Stadium—not only to run in shorts around a track, but to receive the most scientific training available.

Tom showed Eric how to leave the starting holes sooner, how to bring down his knees a bit, and how to cross the finish line most effectively. Most importantly, Tom told Eric not to stop running right after he finished a race but to go a little farther and gradually cool down his body. Off the track, he instructed him on what to eat before a race, specifically advising his protégé to avoid heavy, starchy meals. Lastly, he always gave Eric a massage after his workouts and races to soften his strained muscles. McKerchar, a trained masseur, was a vocal proponent of kneading the muscles to soften them, and he focused on Eric's thighs and calves.

In a letter Eric expressed his feelings about his early training days:

> *The exercises seemed unimportant at first, but later one finds out how useful they have been. He [McKerchar] took me in hand, pounded me about like a piece of putty, pushed this muscle this way and that muscle the other way, in order, as he said, to get me into shape. Training is not the easiest thing to do. It is liable to become monotonous.*

While the results of such "monotonous" training

would not be completely revealed until the racing season the following spring, Eric did participate in a few more events that summer before joining his family on the coast of Scotland at Largs, where the Clyde River meets the sea. Largs was just a few miles from Helenburgh, where James Liddell had once been inspired by the Reverend Blair to enter the mission field.

In early July, Eric entered the Triangular International Race at Belfast. There the national teams from Scotland and Ireland would race against their counterparts from England and Wales. On July 9, Eric led the field in the 100-yard event, defeating the favored W. A. Hill of England with a time of 10.4 seconds. A race a week later at West Kirkbride on the northern tip of the Cumbria Lake District proved another victory for the newly acclaimed Scottish harrier.

But the summer was not without a certain spiritual dimension. While at Largs, Eric became a member of the Life Guard Corps, a job he loved since not only did he have easy access to the sand for running sprints, he also had the opportunity to meet young people as a witness for Jesus Christ. That summer he came to develop a technique for dealing with certain "tough" characters who had come to the beach to partake in less than honorable pursuits.

Equipped with a fearless demeanor, Eric would

approach the ringleader, usually a prime physical specimen, with a challenge. "You look pretty strong to me," the rather slight lifeguard opined. "Bet you can run pretty fast."

"On the beach here? Lot faster than any of you Corps fellows with your fancy suits and whistles!" the ringleader usually replied.

Without saying another word, Eric then handed his whistle to a bystander. "Just give us a whistle, will you? Let's see who can reach the jetty down there first." And at that, Eric left the fellow yards behind—but he was waiting at the jetty with his hand extended. "Good race; let's run again sometime," he began. And then he would tell the erstwhile braggart about God's Son, who had given Eric all the strength he would ever need.

By the end of the summer, following several races in August at Edinburgh, the Glasgow *Herald* printed a brief review of Eric's first season in collegiate competition:

Eric H. Liddell. . .is going to be British champion ere long. . .and he might even blossom into an Olympic hero. His success has been phenomenal; in fact, it is one of the romances of the amateur path. Unknown four months ago, he today stands in the forecourt of British sprinters.

By September, however, the champion was back

on his bicycle, pedaling to and from campus, the cheers of the spectators a dim memory.

While track could lay claim to the spring and early summer months, rugby was the sport of the fall at Edinburgh University. Again, Eric's rugby career at Eltham had paved the way for him to make the Edinburgh team, and once again, he delighted at the thrill of being part of such a team sport. Throughout November, the university team played against several rugby clubs from London, but by December, Eric had been chosen to try out for the Scottish national team. Following two well-publicized matches, Eric was chosen for the team, an honor equivalent to a college freshman being selected to play on an Olympics squad.

His tenure on the Scottish team that first year, while noteworthy, didn't turn many heads. He was simply another good player on a team of many shooting stars. By January, Eric was glad to resume his daily routine as student. He had earned a B-plus average so far, a distinct achievement for one who had been an average student at a small boarding school, and he wasn't about to sacrifice his grades for the fun of sport.

By May 1922, Eric and Tom McKerchar had again joined forces at Powderhall Stadium. The strict yet likable trainer all too soon had Eric running laps, practicing starts and baton handoffs, and enduring hours of rigorous massages.

"I wish the first race were here at Powderhall," Eric confided to Tom after one particularly arduous practice. The first race of the season—the University Sports—would be held at Craiglockhart, on a grassy track that inexplicably sloped uphill.

On May 27, 1922, Eric once again proved he could give his best at the most important races. On the grassy track of Craiglockhart, Eric's time of 10.2 seconds in the 100-yard race tied the meet record, while his winning, 21.8-second, 220-yard victory was a Scottish record. To the surprise of track aficionados, Eric also won the middle-distance 440-yard race in 52.4 seconds. Considered a sprinter, Eric had never competed in that event in such an important race.

His summer track season was nothing short of stellar, with impressive wins at the Scottish InterVarsity Sports in June, at Powderhall, and in Glasgow. But September came all too quickly— the month when James and Mary, along with Jenny and Ernest, would return to China.

Thanks to the efforts of Sun Yat-sen, the climate in recent years had been very receptive to Christian missionaries, especially those from Great Britain and Russia. Since the Versailles Peace Conference of 1919, when German rights in the Shantung Province had been awarded to Japan, nationalism had gripped China, most widely expressed by an all-out boycott of all things Japanese. At the same time, China began looking to the West, eager for Western philosophy and know-how.

Yet, as always in China, the horizon was dotted with ominous thunderheads. Sun's Kuomintang (KMT) party, which had been impressed with social progress in the newly established Soviet Union, had accepted under its constitution a faction to be known as the Chinese Communist Party. An anti-Christian movement was springing up within the Communist faction and was gaining support.

James and Mary had been reposted to the French missionary compound of Tientsin, a city that held many depressing memories for Mary. Jenny also had found employment in Tientsin, where she would be a student teacher in the British grammar school's kindergarten class.

As Eric helped them pack, he felt far from his usual self. While Rob would be graduating from medical school in a year and would likely be joining his parents in China, Eric knew in his heart that all of them would not be together again for a long time.

Jenny sensed this, too, but she wasn't going to let Eric dampen everyone's spirits. Dragging him by the hand to her room, Jenny pronounced, "I want you to see what I've had to live with the last two years. Just look under my bed!"

Eric began pulling out box after box filled with

his trophies. Little had he realized that Jenny, at the direction of their mother, had saved every token of his many victories in track and rugby. There were gold watches, cake stands, clocks, silver knives and forks—even flower vases! Little had he realized that Mary had painstakingly polished all the silver items, especially the ones she unselfishly gave away.

Eric rolled over on his back and started laughing and laughing.

"I can't believe you've saved all this—and for what?" he exclaimed, almost out of breath.

"No one will ever a need a gold watch or knife or fork in this family, or any other missionary family, that's why," Jenny answered, also laughing. "But from now on, if you win another race, you find a place for all the cake stands!"

Following yet another tearful parting at Waverley Station, Rob and Eric were once more on their own, though they were far from the shy and insecure little boys who had once "run the gauntlet" at Eltham College. In the fall of 1922, with Rob still in medical school at Edinburgh University, the brothers decided to again become roommates, though this time in a slightly different living situation. Sharing a house with twelve other students at first didn't sound ideal to Eric—until he realized how much like his family's home it was. Under the direction of Dr. Lachlan Taylor and his family, the Edinburgh Medical Missionary Hostel, located at 56 George

Square, became a truly happy home for Rob and Eric. In fact, Eric would live there for almost two years until his departure for the Olympic Games in Paris.

That winter Rob, who had always been more forthcoming about his Christian faith than Eric, took what was for him a routine step. As a member of the Glasgow Students' Evangelical Union (GSEU), he began traveling to various industrial towns as part of a "Manhood Campaign," aimed at evangelizing Scotland's men. Organized the previous year by several students, the GSEU hoped to emulate the tremendous revivals of Dwight L. Moody and Henry Drummond during the late 1800s. A dozen or more student evangelists would go into a town, board at the homes of willing citizens, and conduct three to five public services.

But something was missing from these student-led crusades. The students needed to have a speaker whose name was known in Scotland, someone who would attract a bigger audience. In short, someone who would bring the men out of the taverns and the cinema!

David P. Thomson, known as D. P., a theology student from Glasgow who was spearheading Rob's group, was the first to mention Eric's name. He knew Eric had never spoken in public like this, but there was always a first time.

Hitching a ride on a gasoline truck to Edinburgh,

D. P. found the Taylors' house without much trouble. Rob had told D. P. that he couldn't ask his own brother, so D. P. asked to see Eric. The minute he saw him, his throat went dry. Eric's picture had appeared in all the newspapers, and his name was always linked with the Olympics. Stumbling over his words, D. P. explained that Eric would be the guest speaker for an audience of all men in Armadale, Scotland.

"Do you, er, I mean, could you come and just say a few words? About your faith, I mean, and oh, your running, too—"

Eric looked at the floor for a minute then lifted his head and smiled slowly. He had thought of himself in recent years as a future science teacher in China, not a spellbinding preacher like his father and brother. But at this moment he felt a peace inside that he knew could only come from the Holy Spirit. "All right," he said slowly. "I'll come."

In fact, right before D. P. had approached him, Eric had received this in a letter from Jenny in China: "Fear thou not; for I am with thee: be not dismayed; for I am thy God. Isaiah 41:10. Love, Jenny." Jenny's faith had propelled Eric onto a platform he had once feared more than any InterVarsity meet.

That night in Armadale—April 6, 1923—Eric found he had a gift from God he never knew he possessed. He wasn't much of a speaker, but still the eighty men listened to every word he uttered.

And these were men who weren't used to coming to lectures. Unemployment was high in this working-class town, and many men spent their free time in the local taverns or on board ships for months, far away from the Word of God.

Speaking slowly and quietly, Eric made the men feel like he was having a personal conversation with each one of them. "Do you want to know the God I love? He has given me strength when I thought I had nothing left. And He has given me these words when I thought I couldn't speak."

Eric looked around the room from face to face. "Accept God tonight, and tomorrow you will feel a love you have never known before."

The following morning every newspaper in Scotland reported that the great runner Eric Liddell had taken part the previous evening in an evangelistic service. At the same time, Eric himself felt a stirring in his soul like never before. After that one simple service in Armadale, he had a desire to share God's love with every single soul who would listen. But first, he jotted a quick note to D. P., thanking him for opening this door for him.

Eight days after Armadale, Eric went with D. P. to Rutherglen, where he addressed about six hundred students to kick off an Easter revival. A week or so later, Eric himself became an official member of GSEU. Over the next four years, Eric would speak to thousands throughout Great Britain, men and women who may have come at first to see the celebrated athlete, but who returned time and again to hear his simple message of faith.

As the 1923 track season approached, the season leading to the Olympics, many questioned Eric's commitment to running now that he was in such demand as an evangelist. How would he, touted to be Scotland's best runner in years, compete against the world's best? Editorials in Scottish newspapers proclaimed the question of the season: Was Eric Liddell running only for the Lord?

FIVE

Great Britain, 1923–24

Tom McKerchar slammed down the newspaper in disgust. *If I read one more article like that,* he thought, *I may actually speak to the press for a change!* Tom had made it his policy not to give interviews. *But,* Tom thought, *these writers don't know anything about Eric Liddell.* And Eric was about to prove them wrong—in the venue where tenths of seconds measure greatness, and hundredths may confer awe.

For the third year, Eric made an impressive showing at the University Sports, held in May at Craiglockhart. Despite ingesting a healthy helping of Mrs. Taylor's plum pudding back at George Square, Eric managed to win all three events he entered. He was greeted by the roars of the home crowd when he turned in an amazing time of 10.1

seconds in the 100-yard race.

In early June at the Queens Park Football Club Sports in Glasgow, on a fast track, Eric would add to his growing legend when he ran the 100-yard race in 10 seconds flat. Two weeks of intensive training followed this race in preparation for the much-heralded InterVarsity Sport at Craiglockhart on June 16. But the results were worth the hard work.

After winning the 100-yard race again in 10.1 seconds, Eric went on to set a Scottish record in the 220-yard sprint of 21.6 seconds, a record that would stand until 1960. Later at the same meet, Eric would also win the 440-yard event in a time of 50.2 seconds, beating the reigning champion J. G. McColl by 18 yards. Even Eric's harshest critics acknowledged that his times would likely be a full second faster on a cinder track than they'd been on the slow grass of Craiglockhart.

His final race in June of that summer was the Scottish championships at Hampden Park in Glasgow, where he was heartily cheered on to victory in the 100- and 220-yard events by his friends at the GSEU. Yet despite these successes, the biggest test of the summer was looming just ahead.

Up until the summer of 1923, Eric had raced primarily in Scotland, and as the competition had not always been world-class, Eric's times were considered only average. Now as he prepared for his first race in England, there were those who were doubting Scotland should waste the train fare for him to go. How could such a human windmill win an international race?

The race on July 6 and 7, the British Amateur Athletic Association Championships, was considered one of the most important races before the Olympics. Held at London's Stamford Bridge Stadium, the race would feature a long-awaited duel: Eric Liddell, still considered the fastest man in Scotland, against Harold Abrahams, England's best hope at the Paris Games.

Abrahams, a Cambridge University student, was a supremely talented athlete. A long jumper as well as a sprinter, he had competed at the 1920 games in Antwerp but had been eliminated there in both the 100-meter and 200-meter quarterfinals. Now he had been given another chance for the gold, and his determination to achieve that goal separated him from other Olympians. Raised in a German Jewish family in England, Abrahams felt he had been discriminated against because of his Jewish heritage. *If I could be the fastest man in the world*, he thought, *maybe then I would be treated like everyone else and granted the same level of respect.*

Eric, on the other hand, didn't mind if he were treated differently because of his Christian faith. That just gave him one more opportunity to show God's love—to shake every runner's hand and wish them well, to treat every runner the same, and to never use questionable language or tell off-color jokes. But Eric still wanted to win. If Harold Abrahams wanted to be the best, he would have to beat Eric Liddell.

The stadium at Stamford Bridge was filled to capacity on Friday, July 6, 1923, as the temperature soared to over 90 degrees Fahrenheit. Men were wiping their foreheads with handkerchiefs, while women fanned themselves with paper fans. All eyes were straining to see the runners on the track.

Eric, the shorter of the two at five-foot, nine inches, approached Harold first and shook hands with the tall, dark-haired sprinter. Then they took their positions for the 220-yard race. Earlier that morning, Eric had won his first heat of the 220-yard race in 22.4 seconds. The top three runners of each of the two first heats had advanced to the second heat. Eric knew he would have to get a better start this time because Abrahams, the consummate athlete, was known for his lightning starts.

As Eric dug his holes in the track, he glanced at the other runners. But Harold's eyes were on the track, deep in concentration. Closing his own eyes, Eric prayed silently, thanking God again for giving him this special ability.

One Bible verse always came to him right before a race, one that Eric liked to describe as the "three sevens" because it was from the seventh book of the New Testament (1 Corinthians), the seventh chapter, and the seventh verse: "But every man hath his proper gift of God, one after this manner, and another after that." Yet, despite his God-given talent, Eric never once felt that God granted him special favors to win races.

As the race official came into view, Eric focused all his attention on the track. After carefully placing his toes in the starting holes, he raised his muscular legs and arched his back just the way McKerchar had taught him. Then he waited for the gun.

At the sound of the starting pistol, Abrahams exploded from the line, leading the pack by two yards. Once again, Eric had gotten off to a poor start, and he could feel all eyes on him. Swinging his arms, Eric willed himself forward, closer and closer to Abrahams.

In the stands, Tom McKerchar watched the race almost holding his breath, while a stream of perspiration trickled down his cheek. Suddenly, the red-faced Scottish man seated next to him began jumping up and down. "Look at him now! Aye, he culdna win if his heid's na back!"

As if he had heard his countryman's cry, Eric finally threw his head back, his eyes on the cloudless sky above. Gasps could be heard as the two men pushed to the finish line, each one seeming to throw his chest out farther to gain the advantage. At the tape, Eric Liddell had edged out Harold Abrahams with a win of 21.6 seconds, a blistering pace!

On Saturday, the rumor circulating through the stadium was that Eric and Harold would meet again in the finals of the 100-yard race. Both men had won their first heat of the race—Eric in 10.0 seconds and Harold in 10.2—and now the second heats were about to begin. While Eric set a new British national record in the 100, running the distance in an incredible 9.8 seconds, Harold did not place in the top three of his heat and could not go to the finals.

By the end of the day, Eric had won the 220-yard and the 100-yard events and was awarded the Harvey Memorial Cup as the best British athlete of 1923. His final time of 9.7 seconds in the 100-yard race was another new British record, one that would not be broken for thirty-five years. That time was of crucial importance for the hopes of Great Britain in the Olympics, as it was just a tenth of a second slower than the pace set by American world-record-holder Charley Paddock.

Eric Liddell was now the reigning British champion in two track events, and the press would not let him forget that. On the train back to Scotland, Tom showed Eric the latest newspaper articles. "In a few weeks I've gone from goat to glory," Eric exclaimed, laughing.

"Or from black sheep to world's fastest human," joked Tom. "They're even calling you, and I quote, 'the Scot who would send Paddock packing,' and 'the man to finish what Wyndham Halswelle began.'"

"Good old Wyndham," Eric remembered, smiling. "Now that's something my dad would like to see."

Putting the papers aside, Tom stared out the window for a while. "You know, we won't know for sure about the Olympics until the race at Stoke-on-Trent in a couple weeks." Tom turned to look at Eric, and then playfully punched him in the arm. "But it looks like it's you and me in Paris next summer."

Eric shook his head, laughing. Retrieving his Bible from his satchel, Eric opened the worn leather volume to 2 Corinthians, chapter 10, verse 17: "But he that glorieth, let him glory in the Lord." As the countryside passed in a blur, Eric tried desperately to focus his thoughts.

Following the Stoke-on-Trent race, when Eric was pushed off the track but still managed to win, Eric's celebrity only grew, if that were possible. While the field hadn't included Harold Abrahams, who had bowed out due to a strep infection, Eric's feat was still almost unimaginable. When people would inquire about his physical and emotional resources during that race, Eric's reply was usually the same: "I don't like to be beaten."

And he didn't like to be deterred from his goals. While he played a little rugby during the fall of 1923, Eric concentrated on what he thought would be his final year at Edinburgh University. He had every intention of obtaining his bachelor of science degree in May, and then, following the Paris Games, making his way to Tientsin. He would arrive only six months after his brother, Dr. Robert Victor Liddell, who that winter had begun his medical missionary duties in Fulien, South China.

Letters from Eric's parents seemed to underscore his desire to arrive as soon as possible. They spoke of the efforts of Mao Tse-tung, the scholarly son of a poor peasant, who had recently founded the Chinese Communist Party and was organizing the peasants into a revolt, as a backlash against years of unthinkable poverty and horrible living conditions. The forces of nature seemed to imitate the hostile political climate, with floods, famine, and disease conspiring to create national chaos. *How much worse will the situation be when I arrive?* Eric anguished.

But as the new year arrived in Edinburgh, Eric would face a crisis all his own.

For many days, Tom McKerchar had been checking the mail at the athletic director's office at Edinburgh University. It had been rumored that Baron Pierre de Coubertin, the founder of the modern Olympics and president of the International Olympic Committee, was set to release the racing schedule for the summer Olympics sometime in January. *The schedule for the Olympics should have been sent by now,* he thought anxiously.

He had heard that this summer the baron wanted the Olympics to last only two weeks, and not the entire summer, as in some past competitions. He also knew that no races would be scheduled on Monday, July 14, known in France as Bastille Day, a national holiday.

A soft knock on his office door caused McKerchar to sit up in his chair. "Mr. McKerchar," the athletic director's secretary said, interrupting his thoughts, "I believe it's here." In her hand she waved the official-looking envelope.

Ripping the envelope open, McKerchar scanned page after page of the lengthy schedule. *There it is,* he thought excitedly, *the 100-meter race. And the first heats are on. . .*

The pages slipped through his hands and fell, one by one, gracefully to the floor. He buried his head in his hands for a moment, and then stood, making his way to the door. "I'll be out for a while. I need to catch up with Eric if I can."

Racing back to retrieve the schedule, he then sped out again just as quickly, catching a glimpse of his secretary's surprised face. "And don't tell anyone the schedule is in," he advised sternly. "We don't want reporters hounding Eric—at least, not yet!"

Eric was at George Square, trying to get a few hours of studying in before he left again with D. P. to give another speech. Since Eric had made the British Olympic team, the demand to hear him had only increased. Now he was speaking two or three times a week, gaining confidence each time he made his way to the podium. At times, the crowd was too large for the hall that had been chosen, another indication of Eric's widespread fame. Based partly on his reputation as an evangelist, he had even been invited to participate in the Penn Relays at the University of Pennsylvania in April.

When Tom found Eric, Tom didn't know what to say, but that was never a problem with Eric. With a broad grin on his face, Eric began telling Tom about his travels for the Lord. Tom tried to pay attention, but soon Eric was aware that his mind was elsewhere. "What is it, Tom? If you don't mind, I have to say you don't look well," Eric said, his voice concerned.

Tom cleared his throat. "It's just, Eric, I know what you're going to say—but I wish I could change your mind."

"Out with it, man! Only God can read minds." Eric motioned Tom on with his hand.

"The Olympic schedules came in the mail today. You know, the baron is trying to fit all the events and heats into just two weeks. So—"

"So, what is it, Tom?"

"The first heats for the 100-meter race are to be held on a *Sunday,* Eric. July 6, to be exact."

Without a moment's hesitation, Eric said, "I'm not running." His eyes did not blink, he did not wring his hands, and he did not pace the floor of his room.

Sighing, McKerchar turned away from him and glanced out the window.

"Tom, do you really know why I can't run? God's fourth commandment to Moses said to remember the Sabbath Day to keep it holy. If I run in a race that honors me or other men, I am not remembering God's Sabbath. And if I start ignoring one of God's commands, I may as well ignore all of them. But I can't do that because I love God too much."

McKerchar nodded his head. Eric had never raced on a Sunday, and he wouldn't change his beliefs now, even for the Olympics. "I'll contact the British authorities; that's the next step," he said. "But Eric, are you ready for what will happen? I mean, the reporters?"

"Jesus never said that to follow Him would be easy," Eric answered simply.

In the weeks that followed, McKerchar and the British sports authorities tried desperately to change the date of the first heats. The French officials, however, refused to comply. Instead, Eric was entered in the 200- and 400-meter races, events that he had won before but that he clearly did not dominate. Two other relay events—the 4 x 100 and the 4 x 400—were not considered because their heats also fell on a Sunday.

And in the weeks that followed, the attacks by the British press were nonstop. "A traitor to Scottish sporting, to all that Wyndham Halswelle stood for!" proclaimed one paper. Another journalist reported that Eric was not running so he could get more publicity. Time and again, the papers questioned why Eric couldn't run on Sunday and dedicate the race to the Lord.

Eric was disappointed, but he never wavered in his decision. Besides, such a stand by an athlete was hardly a new issue. In the 1900 Olympics, also held in Paris, several athletes decided not to participate when the heats for many events were scheduled on a Sunday. In the 1908 London Games, a theology student from the United States named Forrest Smithson protested against Sunday trial heats by running the 100-meter hurdles with a Bible in his hand.

But to make matters worse, a British noble was quoted as saying, "To play the game is the only thing in life that matters." Eric Liddell had decided he would play the game, but only on God's terms.

All through the winter and spring, McKerchar and Eric trained harder and harder for the two events he would run, and they were especially gratified to learn that lanes would be used in the 400-meter event to prevent a repeat performance of the Stoke-on-Trent race. While the Olympics was at the top of their agenda, it was by no means their only focus. The track season had once again arrived in Edinburgh, inaugurated as always by the University Sports.

At Craiglockhart, Eric tied the meet record for the 100-yard race, with a time of 10.2 seconds. He went on to win the 220-yard race and then broke the meet record for the 440-yard event, crossing the finish line in 51.5 seconds. At Hampden Park in Glasgow, he repeated his performance at the Scottish InterVarsity Sports, winning all three events. But the most important race before the Paris Games would be held on a weekend in late June in London. While it was assumed that Eric would be an integral part of the British Olympic team, he still had to qualify in his two events.

On Friday night, June 21, in just three-and-a-half hours, Eric won two heats in the 220-yard race and two heats in the 440-yard event. On Saturday, he faced off against true world-class competition in the finals of both events. Eric would finish second in the 220, after A. O. Kinsman of South Africa, and would win the 440, with a time of 49.6 seconds. The latter time was of significance: First, Eric's time was better than the existing Olympic record for the 400-meter race, which was a full stride shorter that the 440; and, in keeping with the Scots' reverence for Wyndham Halswelle, Eric's time was a second slower than the famed runner's British and Scottish record for the quarter mile.

With the Olympics less than a month away, the British team was now in place. Eric Liddell had made a decision not to sacrifice his faith for the glory of winning, a decision that might affect the medal count for Great Britain. As he prepared to leave for Paris, Eric sought solace in God's Word and found particular comfort in one verse: "Whosoever believeth on him [God] shall not be ashamed" (Romans 10:11).

To him, God meant more, much more, than an Olympic gold medal.

SIX

Paris, 1924

No other sports competition has driven athletes to train harder than the Olympics. Perhaps one reason is that the Olympics has a tradition like no other sports event, with a history that can be traced back to 776 B.C.

From that date until A.D. 394, the Olympian games were held in the summer every four years—known as an "olympiad"—at Olympia, Greece. These games were the most famous of four ancient Greek national festivals, the others being the Isthmian, Pythian, and Nemean games. Only honorable men of Greek descent could participate in the Olympian games.

Olympia was not a town but rather a sanctuary with buildings constructed strictly for the worship of the gods. Almost resembling a museum, the ancient site was also home to many treasures of Greek art, monuments, altars, statues, and theaters. The most celebrated building or temple at Olympia was the Temple of Zeus, dedicated to the "father" of the Greek gods. And it was in the sanctuary of Zeus that the games were held.

The order of events is not known, but it is assumed that the first day of the ancient Olympian games was devoted to the offering of sacrifices to the gods. Following those offerings, the contestants stood in front of an ivory and gold statue of Zeus and took an oath vowing honesty and fairness.

The second day began most likely with footraces, an event that could be viewed in the *stadion*, an oblong area that was the predecessor of modern stadiums. On the following days wrestling, boxing, and the *pancratium*, a combination of the two, were held. Horse racing came next, followed by the pentathlon, a series of five athletic tests, including sprinting, long jumping, javelin hurtling, discus throwing, and wrestling.

The closing event of the Olympian games was a race between men wearing suits of armor. Whoever won that race was crowned by the high priest of Zeus with a wreath made from wild olive branches and leaves. After a poem was read that had been written to celebrate his victory, the winner was carried home to his native village on the shoulders of his friends. For the rest of his life, he would be treated like an emperor—in other words, everything he wanted would be given to him, at no charge.

For more than a thousand years, the Olympic games continued like this until, for some unknown reason, the Roman emperor Theodosius I did away with the competition. But in the late 1800s, as people again became interested in studying about ancient Greece, the French sportsman and educator Baron Pierre de Coubertin decided to bring back the games as a worldwide sports competition. To spark interest in such a spectacle, he loved to tell the story of how a Greek soldier named Pheidippides ran from Marathon to Athens in full armor to bring the news of victory over the Persians. Before dropping dead on the spot, Pheidippides is supposed to have cried, "Rejoice, we conquer!" The facts of this story cannot be proven, yet the sheer romance of it and other Greek tales of courage were enough to generate vast public support.

Since 1896, when the games were again held in Greece, the Olympics have continued to be held every four years—except during the two world wars—but in different locations. And since 1912, women have been allowed to compete as well, although none participated in track and field events until the summer games of 1928. The Winter Olympics, which were instituted in 1924, were held in the same year as the Summer Olympics until 1994, when it was decided the winter games would alternate with the summer games in even-numbered years.

The 1896 games, held in April, were particularly notable because of a dispute that arose between the city of Athens and Baron de Coubertin. Citing the history of the Olympics, the Athenians wanted to be the permanent hosts of the games, but Coubertin adamantly refused, citing the need to develop international support for the competition. In protest, Athens played host to their own games in 1906, as a way of marking the tenth anniversary of the modern games. These games became known as the Intercalated Games of 1906 and were not officially sanctioned by the International Olympic Committee. Coincidentally, it was at the 1906 games that Wyndham Halswelle created such a stir, becoming the first Scot to win a medal in Olympic track and field competition.

In 1924, the eighth Olympic Games of modern times promised to be the greatest sporting event in the history of the world. The numbers alone supported this boast: Forty-four countries were to send more than three thousand athletes to compete in Paris, including four hundred from the United States alone, the largest contingent, and two from China.

Baron de Coubertin was so thrilled to have the games in his city of Paris that he selected a special motto for that Olympic year, one actually taken from a French football (soccer) team. The motto "Citius, Altius, Fortius!" (meaning, "Faster, Higher,

Stronger!") was coined, ironically, not from the Greek but from Latin.

Who would be the strongest, who would jump the highest, who would run the fastest race?

Among those competing for the gold in 1924 besides Eric Liddell and Harold Abrahams were the "Flying Finns" Paavo Nurmi and Ville Ritola (long-distance runners); the New Yorker Gertrude Ederle (swimming); the future Tarzan of film, Johnny Weissmuller (swimming); Duke Kahanamoku (swimming); the father of film star Grace Kelly, Jack Kelly Sr. (rowing); and the renowned pediatrician Dr. Benjamin Spock (rowing).

While the British team boarded a modest steamer for the trip across the English Channel early that first week of July, their entrance paled beside the arrival of the powerhouse team from the United States. Those American athletes not affiliated with the navy arrived on the ocean liner SS *America,* while the navy men arrived proudly on a battleship. A 200-meter cork track had been laid on the deck of the *America* for the United States track team to practice while crossing the Atlantic. Nearly all the members of the British team were university students, who were traveling at their own expense; for the first time ever, a few of the neediest athletes had been given financial assistance.

Still, no one was discounting the chances of the British track team to bring home Olympic gold.

Saturday, July 5, 1924. *Today it all begins,* Eric thought as he gazed at his reflection in the window of a storefront. And not only his reflection, but the identical images of many members of the British Olympic team, who were all dressed alike. Eric and the team—decked out in cream-colored skirts and pants, blue blazers, and white straw hats—were awaiting the signal to begin marching down the Champs-Elysees, the grand boulevard of Paris, and then on to the Olympic stadium, known in Paris as the *Stade Colombes.*

Taking his handkerchief from his jacket pocket, he wiped away a stream of perspiration from the side of his face. The temperature in Paris was already in the nineties, with an expected high of 110 degrees Fahrenheit.

Eric filed into line next to Douglas Lowe, his roommate in Paris and one of the favorites to win a medal in the 800-meter race. Just ahead of him was Harold Abrahams, voted captain of the British track team. More than many runners, Abrahams had understood why Eric couldn't run on Sunday. Because he wanted others to respect his Jewish faith, he, in turn, respected Eric for taking such a brave stand.

At the Arc de Triomphe, the parade of athletes paused while Britain's Prince of Wales (later King Edward VIII) placed a wreath at the Tomb of the Unknown Soldier, a monument dedicated to those who had died in World War I.

But Eric felt his heart skip a beat at the entrance to the Olympic stadium. More than sixty thousand spectators filled the stands, and the sound of their applause was like the roar of many oceans, filling his ears. Nation after nation marched under the "Marathon Gate" into the stadium, led by the first team, the athletes from South Africa. Each team was preceded by its nation's flag and sometimes by a band from that country.

Just before Eric and the British team entered, the Queen's Cameron Highlanders began to play their bagpipes and beat their drums to the soulful lament, "The Flowers of the Forest." Dressed in Scottish kilts and wearing bearskin headdresses, the Highlanders held special meaning for Eric, but he hoped their mournful musical selection wasn't an omen for the days ahead. He knew he had disappointed Scotland by refusing to run in the 100-meter race. But he still had two races to run. . . .

Finally, Baron de Coubertin gave a short speech, and military bands played the French national anthem, "La Marseillaise." Cannons boomed as the Olympic flag with its five rings rose into the sky. The eighth Olympics had officially begun.

Sunday, July 6, 1924. As Eric made his way to the pulpit of the Scots Kirk, the Scottish Presbyterian church in Paris, Harold Abrahams began digging his holes in the cinder track for the first 100-meter heat. The 100-meter race was considered the test for the world's fastest human. From the United States, world-record-holder Charley Paddock and his teammate Jackson Scholz were considered the favorites; from New Zealand, Art Porritt was considered a possible medalist; and from Great Britain, Abrahams alone carried the hopes of his nation.

As Eric arrived back at his hotel in the afternoon, an exhausted Harold was receiving his victory massage from his trainer Sam Mussabini. Mussabini was almost as legendary a figure as his protégé, having trained Willie Applegarth, the bronze medalist in the 200 meters at Stockholm (1912), and Harry Edward, the 200-meter bronze medalist at Antwerp (1920). Harold had made it through two heats and was ready to run the final on Monday.

Monday, July 7, 1924. Eric tried to ignore the stares from the crowd as he found his seat in the Olympic stadium. He did not have a race to run today, a fact the newspapers had all reported at great length. But he did have a race to watch and a runner to cheer—the tall and muscular Harold Abrahams.

Four Americans were also in the 100-meter final, including the favorite, Paddock, and Scholz from the University of Missouri, considered almost his equal. Paddock still held the Olympic record of 10.8 seconds, set at Antwerp in 1920.

Eric squinted his eyes and cupped his hands over his forehead so he could see better. *Abrahams looks as determined as ever,* he thought. Eric joined in the cheering until the race official held up his gun.

At the sound of the blast, the runners sprang to life, soaring down one length of the track. With Scholz at his heels, Abrahams fought for the lead, breaking the finish line first. He had run his best race ever that day, setting a new Olympic record—10.6 seconds—and had won the gold medal. Porritt of New Zealand edged out American Chester Bowman for the bronze medal.

Jumping up and down in the stands, Eric was happier than most of the excited fans there. In his heart, he knew this had been God's plan. He was to give God glory in his way, as a Christian, and Harold Abrahams was to show his God-given talent in another. (Abrahams was the first British runner to win a gold medal at the Olympics—no European runner would win this event again until the 1980 Olympics—and he intended to savor the victory for the rest of his life. Until his death in 1978, every year on the seventh of July, at precisely 7:00 P.M., the time of the 100-meter final at the 1924 games, Abrahams and his wife, along with Art Porritt and his wife, sat down to a commemorative dinner.)

Tuesday, July 8, 1924. Tom McKerchar and Eric shared a taxi to the Olympic Stadium, but their ride was silent. *Today is the day*, Tom thought, *for Eric to prove all those reporters wrong*. His face catching the breeze from the open window, Eric thought, *Today is the day for me to run my race.*

As they walked around the track, McKerchar shook his head. "It doesn't look good, Eric. They've just laid new cinders, and the track is not packed very tightly. Times should be slower."

"Not to mention the heat! Now I know why my ancestors settled in Scotland," Eric answered lightly. "And please don't look so serious, Tom. This is why I run—to be in races like this."

Shaking his head, McKerchar found his seat in the stands as Eric joined the other runners for the first heats of the 200-meter race. Later, both men were proved right. The times for all the top runners were slower, but all the top runners, including Harold Abrahams, came through. The stage was set for Wednesday's 200-meter semifinal and final races.

Wednesday, July 9, 1924. As temperatures again soared into the hundreds, Eric found his place on the track for his semifinal race. In the 200-meter race, runners would make one turn, covering exactly half of the oval track.

Eric knew this race might be as tough as the

final, if he made it there. To his left was the great American runner, Charley Paddock. Paddock had finished in fifth place in the 100-meter race, and it was clear he wanted revenge. Abrahams had run in the first semifinal of the day and barely made it to the finals with a third-place finish. Eric acknowledged his friend on the sidelines with a wave. He knew he couldn't let Abrahams alone carry the British team into the finals.

At the start of the gun, Paddock leaped ahead of Eric, until Eric put his arms in motion. Then, for a few strides, the men ran side by side. At the finish tape, Paddock edged out Eric, winning the semifinal in 21.8 seconds, just one-tenth of a second faster than the Scottish runner. Eric had made it to the finals—but could he run this hard again?

The finals for the 200 meters were to be held in the late afternoon, but the lane assignments were posted soon after the semifinals. Abrahams would be in lane two, the second from the most inside lane; Scholz was in lane four; Eric had been given lane five; and Paddock was in the most outside lane, lane six. All in all, six runners had made it to the finals.

As the race began, Eric doubted he had the energy to finish in the top three. Paddock got off to a fast start, followed closely by Scholz. Abrahams was somewhere behind Eric, the heat having sapped his strength, as well. Remembering McKerchar's advice, Eric pumped his knees higher and threw out his chest. At the finish line, Eric had edged out two runners to gain third place. He had won the bronze medal.

Eric had become the first Scot in Olympic history to win a medal in the 200 meters, and the first Scot to win any medal since the famed Wyndham Halswelle in 1906. Even the newspapers were kind to him, with *The Scotsman*, in a story entitled "Thrilling Olympic Finishes," reporting, "As usual, Liddell did not start too well but made a wonderfully fast finish."

After hugging McKerchar and Abrahams at the same time, Eric quickly made his way down the stairs to the dressing rooms, located below the stadium. There would be no victory laps, no flag waving, no fist pumping. That was not Eric's style.

But tomorrow he would be back on the cinder track. Back to prove he could still run the 400-meter race, even though he was far from the favorite.

SEVEN

Paris, 1924

Friday, July 11. Outside the Hotel Moderne Eric waited, pacing back and forth. He was to meet McKerchar and a few other British runners there so they could arrive at the same time at the stadium. After Thursday's heats, he seemed to feel every muscle of his body. He had run more races in a few days than he had in a month!

Then Eric saw a familiar face. Running up to him was the masseur the British team had hired just for the Olympics. Occasionally, he had helped McKerchar give Eric a massage. Eric extended his hand and patted the older man on the back. But the masseur said only a few words and handed Eric a small piece of paper that had been folded once. Then he turned just as quickly to go.

"Thanks, I'll read it at the stadium!" Eric called to him, puzzled that the man hadn't wanted to have a conversation. Shrugging his shoulders, Eric put the paper in his pocket. And then it was forgotten as McKerchar and the others greeted him.

As if by tacit agreement, no one spoke of Thursday's heats. While Eric had won his first heat with a time of 50.2 seconds and had finished second to Adrian Paulen of the Netherlands in the second, he would still have to improve his times by at least a second to even figure in the medals. With each heat, it seemed, the runners were raising the bar of excellence in the 400-meter event.

After the semifinal heats—the third heats—had been run Friday afternoon, six runners had qualified for the final 400-meter race, to be held at 6:30 that evening. The favorites were two Americans: Horatio Fitch and J. C. Taylor. Joseph Imbach of Switzerland and D. M. Johnson of Canada were also contenders. Guy Butler, Britain's silver medalist at Antwerp in this event, was still in the race, but he had injured his leg. With his thigh heavily bandaged, he would not be able to crouch down into the traditional starting position.

And then there was Eric. He had been given lane six for a starting position, the dreaded outside position.

As he plopped down in a chair in the dressing room, Eric had never felt so tired. *In just two hours*

I'll have to run the race of my life, he thought desperately. Reaching inside his coat pocket, he happened upon the paper given to him hours before. Unfolding the now crumpled square, Eric quickly read the message. Then, bowing his head, Eric whispered, "Thank You, God."

Written with care, the message read, "In the Old Book it says, 'For them that honour me I will honour.' Wishing you the best of success always." The verse quoted was 1 Samuel 2:30, a verse Eric himself had always loved. Yes, he had always tried to honor God, even though he was far from perfect. And while others might think that he expected God to help him win the 400-meter race that evening, Eric knew God had blessed him in countless ways already.

As 6:30 approached, Eric laced on his leather running shoes and walked slowly up the stairs to the familiar cinder track. Deafening cheers arose from the crowd at the sight of the runners, especially the Americans Fitch and Taylor. The stars and stripes of the American flag were waving everywhere Eric looked.

Nudging Guy Butler with his elbow, Eric joked, "Has someone forgotten to tell them that two Brits are still in the race?"

Guy tried to smile. "Look at me, Eric. They know I'll never win with this leg, even if I give it all I have. Besides, this is Fitch's event—he'll be trying to beat his own Olympic record." Just that afternoon Fitch had won his semifinal heat with a time of 47.8 seconds, a new Olympic record.

The time for the runners' warm-ups around the track dwindled as the race official in his long white coat approached the cinder oval. But just at that moment, the blaring of horns and the pounding of drums could be heard from outside the Marathon Gate, the formal entrance to the stadium.

The Queen's Cameron Highlanders had arrived, and no official could stop them from marching around the track! Dressed in their full costume—Scottish kilts and bear-skin headdresses—they proceeded to play the traditional Scottish "fight" song, "The Campbells Are Coming."

Eric and Guy couldn't believe their ears or their eyes. All around them, Union Jacks began flying, the symbol of their country. Now the British fans were on their feet cheering, even as the last wail of a bagpipe faded into the night air.

In the minutes that followed, Eric once again went from runner to runner, extending his hand and wishing them well. The Cameron Highlanders had postponed his ritual, one that he had never forgotten. After all these races, the runners had even come to expect this from Eric. To their amazement, he seemed to mean what he said, too.

Clearing his throat, the race official then extended his arm, the pistol pointed to the heavens.

All the runners were in their starting positions, all except Guy Butler, who was almost standing. Eric looked ahead to the first curve of the track. He knew what he had to do. There was only one way he would win this race. And only God could help him succeed.

In the stands, McKerchar held his stopwatch firmly in his hand. As the gun went off, he set the timepiece in motion, his eyes fastened on the track. And then his jaw dropped. Eric was sprinting to the first turn, leading all the runners by more than three meters! McKerchar blinked his eyes and looked back quickly. And not only that, Guy Butler, bad leg and all, was in second place, his face wrinkled with pain.

Checking his stopwatch halfway through the one-lap race, McKerchar clocked Eric at 22.2 seconds. At that pace, Eric would have won most 200-meter races. No 400-meter runner in his right mind would run that fast and still have enough stamina left to finish strong. And then the seasoned trainer saw what he knew would happen: Horatio Fitch had just passed Guy Butler, and his pumping fists were propelling him toward Eric!

Farther back in the pack, Taylor and Imbach, eager to change lanes, had both stumbled briefly. They were now well behind Johnson, Butler, Fitch, and Eric, who was still hanging on to a slim lead.

Now in the final stretch, McKerchar, in spite

of himself, began pumping his own fists, imitating Eric. There he was, his face to the sky, arms flailing like twin windmills, knees pumping almost to his chest, with the finish tape in sight. Sensing Fitch near him, Eric doubled his efforts, widening the gap between them.

Eric Liddell of Scotland broke the finish tape of the 400-meter race at the 1924 Olympic games, running at the world-record pace of 47.6 seconds! He was five meters ahead of Horatio Fitch, and Guy Butler had bravely finished third.

Clutching his sides, Eric slowed to a stop. He had nothing left to give. After a few minutes, he slowly turned around and walked up to Horatio Fitch and extended his hand and then went over to congratulate Guy Butler, who had collapsed on the grass.

As the band began playing "God Save the Queen," McKerchar raced toward Eric, his arms extended. "You couldn't just win, you had to set a world record!" he cried out above the crowd's cheers.

Turning to the crowd, Eric waved briefly. At the end of the race, he had not seen the finish tape, but he had seen hundreds of Union Jacks waving wildly. And now he had brought home the gold medal, the first ever won by a Scotsman. He was not proud of himself, but he was proud of his country.

The following day, Eric was in his hotel room working on another speech he was to give Sunday at the Scots Kirk. He had left the stadium as quietly as he could shortly after the race to begin writing, and besides, he hadn't wanted to talk to too many reporters. At the 1924 games, there was no medal ceremony, no moment when the top three finishers stood on a festooned platform, tears streaming down the face of the victor as his country's national anthem was played. Rather, the gold, silver, and bronze medals were mailed to the athletes several weeks after the games.

But now a knock on the door caused Eric to put down his pen. "Tom, I had a feeling you might drop by," he greeted his friend.

McKerchar was holding an armful of newspapers, a smile lighting up his face. "In case you have any doubts, you're an official Scottish hero!"

Teasing him, Eric began to push Tom out the door. "I don't want to know anymore, Tom. Wasn't it bad enough when I was the next Wyndham Halswelle?"

"Aye, that it was. But now you're the next Rob Roy and William Wallace [two legendary Scottish heroes] rolled into one! Listen to this," he continued, reading from the London paper. " 'No longer a traitor to his country, Eric Liddell is the greatest quarter-miler ever!' "

Perusing a copy of *The Scotsman*, McKerchar regaled the Olympic hero with this tribute: " 'The greatest achievement in the Olympic Games so far has been accomplished by a Scotsman,'" he read in a solemn voice. "'This is the crowning distinction of Liddell's great career on the track, and no more modest or unaffected world champion could be desired.' Sit down a minute, I'm not through!" McKerchar was distracted by Eric's methodical pacing.

"The best is yet to come—first a quote from the distinguished Harold Abrahams. And I read, 'People may shout their heads off about his appalling style. Well, let them; he gets there.'" At that, both McKerchar and Eric broke up laughing.

"That is good, Tom. I'll have to come up with a fitting tribute for him, too."

McKerchar cleared his throat and wiped his eyes. "And now a quote from the Flying Scotsman himself."

Eric groaned loudly. He had hesitated saying anything to the press for fear his words would sound too proud. But he did want to share his faith in some way. That was why he had come to Paris in the first place.

"'The secret of my success over the 400 meters,' Mr. Liddell explained, 'is that I run the first 200 meters as hard as I can. Then, for the second 200 meters, with God's help, I run harder.' Spoken like a real hero, if I may say so myself," McKerchar added.

A few days later, after crossing the English Channel from France to England, the British

Olympic team boarded a train for London's Victoria Station. A tumultuous welcome awaited as crowds surrounded Eric when he descended the platform. They then joined the parade as he was carried on the shoulders of his fellow Scotsmen to his next train— the one that would take him home to Edinburgh. At Waverley Station, the scene was repeated as Scots welcomed their native son.

At the 1924 Olympics, Eric Liddell had indeed been "Citius, Altius, Fortius"—but he had also been much more. He had run one race and received the ultimate prize. Now God was calling him to a greater race, one in which there would be no medals and no applause.

EIGHT

Edinburgh, 1924–25

None of Eric's family had been in attendance at *Stade Colombes*, and none of his family would witness his college graduation. But their absence, while keenly felt by Eric, would be compensated for by a legion of dignitaries, college classmates and professors, and Scots. On July 17, 1924, the date of Eric's commencement, a surprise ceremony had been planned that would rival those Olympian homecomings of ancient Greece.

Edinburgh University's McEwan Hall was packed to overflowing as members of the audience fought for a clear view of the stage. Yet because there were no microphones and no sophisticated sound system, the audience was eerily silent, hanging on every word of the graduation marshals. One by one, the graduates' names were read, and one by one, the students solemnly received their hard-earned diplomas. And then came the announcement the crowd had so eagerly awaited.

"The bachelor of science degree, Mr. Eric Henry Liddell," the marshal announced as Eric ascended the steps of the stage. The audience leaped to their feet, clapping and cheering wildly for their very own hero. For minutes this display of affection continued, until the vice-chancellor, Sir Alfred Ewing, called for silence.

"Mr. Liddell," Sir Alfred began, addressing Eric, "you have shown that none can pass you but the examiner!" Laughter and cheering again erupted at the outrageous pun. Again, Sir Alfred requested order. "In the ancient Olympic tests, the victor was crowned with wild olive by the high priest of Zeus, and a poem written in his honor was presented to him. A vice-chancellor is no high priest, but he speaks and acts for the university; and in the name of the university, which is proud of you and to which you have brought fresh honor, I present you with this epigram in Greek, composed by Professor Mair, and place upon your head this chaplet of wild olive."

Because olive trees do not grow in Scotland, a crown of oleaster sprigs, fresh from the Royal Botanical Gardens of Edinburgh, was placed on Eric's head. Of course, Eric could not be serious at a moment like this, and his infectious smile incited the audience to wild cheering once more. When order was again achieved, Professor Mair proceeded to read his Pindaric ode, patterned after those composed in the fifth century BC to honor the champions at Olympia:

> *Happy is the man who the wreathed games*
> *essaying*
> *Returns with laurelled brow,*
> *Thrice happy victory thou, such speed displaying*
> *As none hath showed 'til now;*
> *We joy, and Alma Mater, for thy merit*
> *Proffers to thee this crown:*
> *Take it, Olympic Victor. While you wear it*
> *May Heaven never frown.*

At the conclusion of the graduation ceremony, his oleaster crown in place, Eric was carried out of McEwan Hall on the shoulders of his fellow students. The procession then made its way to St. Giles Cathedral, considered the Westminster Abbey of Scotland and the birthplace of the Presbyterian church, for a thanksgiving service honoring the graduates. But the service was quickly interrupted by cries for a speech from the man of the moment, Eric Liddell.

Thoughts racing through his mind, Eric acceded to their request and ascended to the podium. "Over the gate at the University of Pennsylvania there is a motto," he began, adjusting his voice to reach the audience of three hundred. "It reads, 'In the dust of defeat as well as in the laurels of victory there is a glory to be found if one has done his best.' There are many men and women who have done their best, but who have not succeeded in gaining the laurels of victory. To them, as much honor is due as to those who have received these laurels." Even amid such overwhelming adulation, Eric remained the modest and unassuming champion.

From St. Giles, Eric was driven to the graduation luncheon at the University Union. It was unusual, indeed unthinkable, for a bachelor of science recipient to be the honored guest at such an affair, but Edinburgh University, nay, Scotland, had never before laid claim to an Olympic gold medalist. Again, Eric's modest humor was on display when he was asked to make a few remarks.

"I ask you to remember today that I suffer from a certain defect of constitution," he said with a wry grin. "I am a short-distance runner, a sprinter, because I suffer from short-windedness, and therefore I will not detain you for long." Laughter greeted his words.

"The papers have told you that my form, my action, is extremely bad," he continued, "but this condition can probably be traced to my forefathers. As we all know in Scotland, the Borderers used to visit England now and then and escape back as quickly as possible. . . . The speed with which my forefathers returned from England seems to have been handed down in my family from generation to generation. They had to get back as best they could, and one did not look for correct action. So this probably explains my own running action."

Following the luncheon, another surprise was in store for Eric, one provided by the University "Blues," or lettermen, of which he was a member. The Blues had procured a carriage with spoked wheels—a hero's chariot, no less—and had decorated it with ribbons of blue and white. In place of horses, several of the university's most muscular athletes pulled the transport, carrying Eric and Sir Alfred to the vice-chancellor's home where tea would then be served. Even Sir Alfred commented that he had never witnessed such a spectacle, nor had he ever basked in such glory.

In the week that followed graduation, Eric was glad for the opportunity to decline several invitations in the interest of running. Because so many world-class athletes from the United States were still in Europe, a special relay meet had been scheduled at Stamford Bridge in London. Teams composed of the best runners on both sides of the Atlantic would compete in a 4 x 400 relay event. The U.S. team had won this event in Paris, and Britain's team had taken the bronze medal (without Eric, who had refused to run on Sunday when the heats for this event were held).

Eric joined fellow Brits Edward J. Toms, Richard N. Ripley, and Guy Butler on the British team, while the United States was represented by Bill Stevenson, E. C. Wilson, R. A. Robertson, and Horatio Fitch. After three laps, the Americans had given their final runner, Fitch, a six-yard lead over Eric, who appeared slightly sluggish. One hundred yards later, Eric was still lagging behind; at the 200-yard mark, he had gained two yards on Fitch. At the 300-yard mark, Eric's trademark windmill style went into full gear, his head went back, and his arms began pumping harder and harder. With fifty yards to go, he pulled even with Fitch and then sped past him, finishing four yards ahead of the great American runner. The British team had beaten the world's fastest 4 x 400 relay team!

For Eric, the remainder of the summer of 1924 dissolved into a succession of running meets, laudatory luncheons, and evangelistic engagements. At one engagement in Edinburgh where he was given an engraved gold watch, a gift from the City of Edinburgh, Eric took special pains to praise Tom McKerchar, who was also in attendance. "It's hard to believe that three years have passed since he tapped me on the shoulder at Powderhall," he reminisced. "But I owe him more than I can describe today. Only God could have provided such a trainer, one who not only brought out my best running, but who supported my faith." When Eric finished, the applause of those present was directed toward Edinburgh University's selfless trainer.

Before going to Paris, Eric had made the decision to attend, and to live at, the Scottish Congregational College in Edinburgh for one year to prepare for the ministry—and his missionary work in China. When he left the following summer, he would lack only a preordination term that he would satisfy when he returned home on his first furlough. His parents, though disappointed that he wouldn't be joining them as soon as they thought, nevertheless fully supported his decision.

Clearly, it was God's will that he remain in Scotland, as evidenced by Eric's impact on three young lives. A young Scot named Peter Marshall was so moved by Eric's words at a rally one summer night that he wrote to both the London Missionary Society and the Scottish Congregational College. Rejected by both, Peter recalled Eric's words, that God has a way of hiding triumphs under tragedies. Later, Peter Marshall went to America, where he would graduate from Atlanta's Columbia Theological Seminary and go on to become a well-respected Christian pastor, who served as chaplain of the United States Senate.

That summer Annie Buchan, a nurse from Peterhead, was inspired by Eric to apply for missionary service in China. Little did she realize that a year later their paths would cross again. For now,

Annie's desire was to work at the mission hospital in Siaochang, the site of Eric's earliest years, where Dr. Robert Liddell was now stationed.

Finally, Eric was the inspiration of Elsa McKechnie, a fourteen-year-old student at George Watson's Ladies' College. Every day she scoured the newspapers for news of her hero; every day she bicycled to the Congregational College in hopes of catching a glimpse of him. When the idea came to her to start an Eric Liddell fan club, she had no trouble finding members among her classmates. Still, she decided to write Eric and ask his permission first.

Eric, being who he was, couldn't refuse, although he did add in his letter, "I don't know what I'm letting myself in for." That was without doubt an understatement, judging from the strict rules of the fan club, which Elsa glowingly shared with him:

1. Each member is entitled to one page of this book, in which a poem or account of Eric Liddell must be inserted, and which must be approved by the committee.
2. Before becoming a member of this club the person in question must undergo an oral examination, given by the founder.
3. Each member must promise these things:

1. Always to uphold Eric Liddell.
2. To attend all meetings arranged by the committee.
3. To keep all rules of the club. It is also desirable that members use the Eric Liddell lines.
4. Members will be presented with a photo of Eric Liddell and must promise to put it in a place of honor.
5. Should any member of this club do anything unworthy of the club, the committee will at once expel the member in question.

After the club was formed, Eric accepted an invitation from Elsa to come to her home for tea, a reply that sent her into a delighted frenzy. Indeed, the McKechnie home was so welcoming and so like his parents' that Eric visited several times during his final year in Edinburgh.

By the fall of 1924, the GSEU campaigns were in full force and Eric was the centerpiece of many, speaking in Androssan, Kilmarnock, and Glasgow. Churches, high schools, sporting clubs, and YMCAs all became stops for speaking engagements. Many of the campaigns railed against the evils of drinking, smoking, and gambling, and during these meetings, Eric proved an especially competent speaker. Instead of using scripture—GSEU members had been accused of being Bible-thumpers—he stated that such habits were bad health risks. At the very successful London campaign of April 1925, the men immediately began extinguishing their cigarettes in response to Eric's talk.

The culmination of his final year with GSEU, the Young Life Campaign, was held in Edinburgh. Referring to D. P. Thomson and Eric Liddell, who were the featured speakers, *The Scotsman* gave this report of the evangelistic gathering: "Both men rely not upon emotional fervour at the expense of reason, but on the direct challenge both to mind and heart of intelligent and robust young manhood. . .one is frequently reminded. . .of Henry Drummond forty years ago in his cooperation with [Dwight] Moody."

While few copies of Eric's speeches still exist from those campaign days, one that has survived is especially telling. A week after the Young Life campaign, Eric addressed, in his simple and sincere style, more than a thousand young women and men at St. George's United Free Church in Edinburgh:

> *Are you living up to the standards of Jesus Christ? We are looking for men and women who are willing to answer the challenge Christ is sending out. . . . Have you sought a leader in everyday life? In Jesus Christ you will find a leader worthy of your devotion*

*and mine. I looked for one I could admire, and
I found Christ. I am a debtor, and no wonder
I am a debtor, for He has given me a message
which can only be experienced. . . . The last
time Edinburgh was swept, all Scotland was
flooded. What are you going to do tonight?*

During this farewell year in Scotland, however, Eric was not all things to all people. He was always available to speak before young people and to appear at most track meets. But he drew the line at becoming a celebrity for celebrity's sake, and he did it with a great deal of panache. When one host, considered a "celebrity collector," invited Eric to a chic party, he received a rude awakening. Rather than arrive in a tuxedo, Eric took a page from his Eltham days and came appropriately attired—in a towel.

"Tell the host it's 'Liddell, Knight of the Bath' you're announcing," he told the butler upon crossing the threshold, his eyes sparkling with humor. The host was not amused, but the guests got the message.

For the fifth time in his running career, Eric competed in the University Sports meet in May at Craiglockhart. His busy social and evangelistic life had not dimmed his love of running, and he easily won the 100-, 220-, and 440-yard events. At that meet and throughout the next month, thousands upon thousands thronged to see the great champion perhaps one last time, and he acquiesced to most requests for autographs.

On Saturday, June 27, 1925, Eric appeared in his final track meet in Scotland. At the Scottish AAA Championship at Hampden Park in Glasgow, an event the GSEU hoped to turn into an evangelistic meeting, Eric did not disappoint the twelve thousand fans who had crowded the gates just to see him. The meet was also a showcase for the 1928 Olympic Games, featuring many who would compete on the future British team.

At Hampden Park, Eric won the 100-yard race in 10.0 seconds, edging the nearest runner by inches. Incredibly, his 220-yard victory mark of 22.2 seconds was faster than his bronze-medal time in Paris when he ran only 200 meters. Finally, in the 440-yard race, Eric won with a personal best time of 49.2 seconds, which would convert to a 48.9-second time for a 400-meter race.

When he was presented with the Crabbie Cup at the conclusion of the meet, the award given to the best track-and-field athlete of Scotland for the year, the crowd's roars were deafening. No Scottish athlete since Eric Liddell has won the award so many times—Eric tied for the award in 1922 and won it outright in 1923, 1924, and 1925—and certainly no Scottish athlete has since been so dominant in one sport. At the awards ceremony, Eric's remarks were fittingly brief: "My motto in life has ever been, if a thing is worth doing, it is worth doing well. I leave the track after four years."

A week later, Eric was bound for China.

Hundreds flocked to his departure services in Glasgow and Edinburgh, where Eric shared how his sister had inspired him to go into evangelistic service. Jenny's scripture selection for her brother, which had once propelled him to face eighty men in Armadale, now seemed especially poignant: "Fear thou not; for I am with thee: be not dismayed; for I am thy God."

One Glasgow newspaper couldn't resist printing a cartoon of Eric running in his shorts, tank top, and clergyman's collar. But underneath the drawing was this sentimental verse:

For China now another race he runs
As sure and straight as those Olympic ones
And if the ending's not so simply known
We'll judge he'll make it, since his speed's his own.

When the day came for Eric to leave his beloved Edinburgh, again hundreds met him at his home to bid farewell—and to send him off in style. Awaiting him at his door was a wildly beribboned carriage that was to be pulled not by horses but two teams of college students. As the carriage, with Eric and his four suitcases, made its way down Princess Street, the procession quickly became a parade, with crowds lining the streets for a last, tear-filled glimpse of the Flying Scotsman. At Waverley Station, the scene became almost chaotic, as hundreds more waited with his train.

As the train pulled out of the station, Eric leaned out the window, trying to think of something to say to the adoring Scots who were running alongside the moving cars. He tried shouting, but the noise of the engine and the cheering prevented anyone from hearing him. Not knowing what else to do, Eric began to sing one of his favorite hymns, "Jesus Shall Reign Where'er the Sun," and soon everyone was singing with him! Unknown to him, as the train picked up speed and Eric's blond head disappeared amid the hills in the distance, the crowd continued singing, verse after verse, to the end.

He was alone with his thoughts as the train sped south to London. He had said good-bye to his "family" in Scotland, those thousands who had followed his running career and those thousands whose lives he had changed as an evangelist, and soon he would say hello to his own family in China. What would await him in the land of his birth, the land that had been so unforgiving and yet so desperate for the good news of Jesus Christ?

Eric had some of the answers at hand. Just before leaving Edinburgh, he had received an annual report written by his father, detailing the current state of political life in China and the special challenges facing missionaries. As he perused the pages, Eric couldn't help but feel dismay—and at the same time, an overwhelming sense of peace. God had led him all the way back to China, around every poorly marked lane and across every humanly constructed finish line. God had prepared him physically, mentally, and emotionally for what lay ahead in a country he now only knew from secondhand reports.

At last, the race of his life had begun.

NINE

Tientsin, China, 1925–28

As the Trans-Siberian Railway rattled across the barren steppes of Siberia, on its way from Chelyabinsk to Vladivostok, Eric closed his eyes and lay back against the cushioned seat. His father's report, its pages now dog-eared, had been crammed into his satchel.

The steamer trip he had made from China to England years ago had been nothing like this, he reflected. Conceived of by Tsar Alexander III, and completed in the early 1900s, the Trans-Siberian Railway had figuratively linked two continents, making travel much less arduous. Thus far on his journey, he had taken a ferry across the English Channel, boarded a train from France to Russia, and then found his seat on the Trans-Siberian

Railway, the world's longest train system, where he would traverse the width of Siberia (five thousand miles). From Vladivostok he would board yet another train, an arm of the Trans-Siberian Railway, to northeastern China.

From his father's report, the political situation was apparently in a state of flux, due primarily to what would be known as the Shanghai Incident. In May 1925, foreign police fired on students and workers in Shanghai and Canton who were protesting the treatment of Chinese workers in foreign-owned factories. In fact, in Hong Kong, the strikes continued for the better part of a year. A number of demonstrators were killed, causing antiforeign sentiments to reach a fever pitch—and missionaries to once again fear for their lives. Eric's father groped for words to describe the situation:

> *The grievances of China have been magnified beyond all recognition. So complex is the situation, so varied are the views expressed, so opposite the conclusions reached, so many the solutions suggested, that one staggers beneath the crushing load. A nation is in travail, seeking to reproduce that which will meet all its aspirations. Whether it will do so or not is another question.*

These strikes had been precipitated by the left

wing of the KMT party of Sun Yat-sen, who had died suddenly in March. This wing, otherwise known as the Chinese Communist Party, led by Mao Tse-tung, wanted a complete transformation of society. The right wing of the party, which favored a strong national state, had since Sun's death been governed by Chiang Kai-shek. It was obvious that these two wings were on a path that could only lead to civil war, a conflict that would dictate who would lead China in the years to come.

As the train made its way south into China, Eric's heart began racing. This was the end of July, and for the Christian missionaries and their families, including the Liddells, that meant visiting the coastal town of Pei-tai-ho. A few stops before Tientsin, Eric alighted on Chinese soil, to the delighted shrieks of his mother and Jenny and cheers from his father and younger brother, Ernest. Rob, who had recently been reassigned to the mission hospital at Siaochang, would be joining the family the next day, along with his new wife.

For the next five weeks, Eric would enjoy a mostly idyllic time at the gulf, savoring the company of his family and other missionaries, getting acquainted with fellow teachers from the Anglo-Chinese College, and even preaching occasional church services in place of his father. Typically, two services were held on a Sunday, with the morning service conducted in Chinese and the evening one in English. Although Eric was quite dismayed to discover how much Chinese he had forgotten, it was no surprise to anyone else. James quietly counseled his son to use the vacation time wisely to brush up on his "mother tongue."

Usually on Sundays, Eric was up to his elbows in fun as the favorite Sunday school teacher in Pei-tai-ho. Although the more straightlaced missionaries shuddered when the children's raucous laughter interrupted the solemnity of the day, most were delighted that the children were enjoying themselves in God's house. And no two were enjoying themselves more than Florence and Margaret Mackenzie, the daughters of Canadian missionaries. They had joined the imaginary club of those wouldn't soon forget Mr. Eric Liddell.

Another lifetime member, Annie Buchan, whom Eric had once inspired during his GSEU campaigns, was also vacationing at Pei-tai-ho with some of her Mandarin Chinese language school classmates from Peking. They were full of news of the aftermath of the Shanghai Incident, reporting widespread student unrest in the capital city.

Likewise, the teachers from the Anglo-Chinese College were more than troubled by what was happening in Tientsin as it appeared that the students would be boycotting the college in September.

Although he would be the youngest member of the faculty, not to mention the one with the least teaching experience, Eric decided to voice his opinion of the situation anyway. Throwing caution to the wind, he advised boldly that the school should open regardless of the strike and, surprisingly, the other teachers concurred. But what would really happen in September?

While that stressful thought was never far from the surface, Eric managed to enjoy himself for the few weeks before the school year began. Here at Pei-tai-ho, he was accepted for who he really was, the son of Christian missionaries, and yes, a missionary himself. He had literally been raised by some of these men and women, and he relished their years of selfless service and knowledge of God's Word. Like Eric, they knew they had been called to China.

Missionaries were not a recent arrival to China. Christian missionaries first arrived in the Far East after Marco Polo's discovery of a trade route to China. Among the first to arrive were the Jesuits (Society of Jesus), traditionally scholarly and dedicated men, and among the first to be recognized was Father Matteo Ricci, who arrived in China in 1583 and succeeded in establishing a permanent mission by 1601.

Since the time of Marco Polo, China had been a magnet, drawing traders and missionaries alike— and the Chinese people did not, and would not, distinguish between the two types of foreigners. To the majority of Chinese, Westerners, no matter what their intentions, were simply "foreign devils." From roughly 1600 to 1800, trade flourished between the West and the East while evangelism languished, a trend aided in part by the destructive effect of opium on the Chinese people.

During the early 1800s, however, both Great Britain and the United States were swept up into a period of Christian revival, and missions once again became a priority for several denominations. Despite the danger of the Opium Wars, Western missionaries flocked to China. The Taiping Rebellion, which began in 1850 and raged for fifteen years, was a bizarre revolt that cost many Western missionaries, as well as people of other faiths, their lives. Led by Hung Hsiu-ch'uan, an unemployed peasant who, after reading missionary tracts, believed he was the younger brother of Jesus Christ, the Taipings, as they called themselves, sought to rid China of evil demons, namely Manchus, Taoists, Buddhists, and Confucians. The rebellion was finally quelled by members of the Chinese gentry.

Despite the anti-Western sentiment fueled by the Taipings and the ever-present colonial attitude of Western powers, the missionaries kept coming. In the 1870s, the Reverend James Hudson Taylor began appealing to the London Council of the China Inland Mission Society to send missionaries to the rural people of northern China. The sheer vastness of the country, coupled with the obvious difficulties involved in evangelizing the more metropolitan areas, gave weight to his argument. In 1884, the first large-scale recruitment of missionaries began intentionally at Oxford and Cambridge universities, an effort aimed at sending "missionary-athletes" to China.

It was Taylor's belief that such well-equipped young men—strong mentally and physically—could best reach out to the people living in the hinterlands of China and bring with them the practices of British education. Dozens of young men answered the call, including the renowned "Cambridge Seven," a group of evangelists who were the true role models for D. P. Thomson and Rob and Eric Liddell.

By the end of the nineteenth century, Protestant missionaries had made their presence known in every province of China, though only a small fraction of the Chinese people had been reached. While eight thousand missionaries from a large number of denominations were actively working in China, the vast majority, despite the efforts of the China Inland Mission, were still on the east coast. Thus it was that James Liddell, answering the call at that time, was sent where he was most needed—to Mongolia, an area so in need of the good news.

Now, twenty-five years later, there were more

missionaries than ever in China, but the anti-Western feelings were as hostile as at any other time. Thanks to the Shanghai Incident, the encroachment of foreign influence was again a red-hot issue. And the missionaries, who lived in relative opulence compared to the majority of Chinese in the larger cities, were regarded with disdain.

Indeed, No. 6 London Mission, the Liddells' address in the French enclave of Tientsin, was a wonderfully spacious house, fronted by a tennis court. The average citizen of Tientsin would never have dreamed of owning a house like that. Although he had his choice of bedrooms, Eric decided to move his things into the smaller attic. From there he was afforded a bird's-eye view of the city, from the squalor of the harbor to the gray-brick towers of the Tientsin Anglo-Chinese College. From there he could spend much-needed time in God's Word and in prayer, as a member of the next generation of Christian missionaries in China.

Eric had been born in Tientsin, but he had no memories of the dirty and sprawling city. In the city's Devil's Market, where his parents often ministered, thieves, opium dealers, and forgers traded illegal goods. And from grimy narrow alleyways lined with flimsy shacks, the city's poor traded almost anything for food. Yet in the more than twenty years since Eric had left, Tientsin was beginning to look like the metropolis it was, the second-largest city in China. Electric streetcars with their swinging cables crisscrossed the center of the city, which was also serviced by three rail lines. Three universities were located within the city limits, and literacy was on the rise, helping to create a market for the seven daily newspapers printed in Tientsin.

Tientsin was known locally as the "City of the Heavenly Ford," but few Westerners would have regarded the River Haiho, which ran through the city, as a divine gift. Every year, the muddy, pulsing channel overflowed its banks, causing the homeless population to increase and spreading disease.

There were but a few elegant neighborhoods, and of course these included the British and French enclaves where the missionaries and all Westerners lived. Ten thousand troops from Western nations remained on hand from the Boxer Rebellion to protect Western interests.

At the Anglo-Chinese College, located on Taku Road, Eric would have little to do with the poor of Tientsin. He would be teaching science, religion, and sports to the sons of middle-class and wealthy families. The school's chief administrator, Dr. Lavington Hart, who had founded the college the year Eric was born, believed that by providing a Christian education to the sons of the most successful families, the future of China would be better. But change had taken place in baby steps.

When the first students arrived in 1902 at "The Hall of New Learning," their name for this revolutionary school, they brought with them their own bedrolls, rice bowls, and chopsticks. At least in 1925, those students who boarded at the school arrived with only clothes and books.

The Anglo-Chinese College was one of three intermediate-level schools operated by foreign missionaries, the others being the American Methodist School and the French Roman Catholic School. The school maintained a steady graduation class of forty to fifty students every year, young men who went on to universities in China or the West, or straight into civil service, business, or politics. When Eric joined the faculty, there were twenty-five Chinese teachers and five British, including A. P. Cullen, formerly of Eltham College and a mentor to Eric.

There were also four hundred boarding and day students, all from non-Christian homes, scheduled to come back or begin school in September. The first day, 150 students showed up; a week later, 300 were in attendance. Eric's "wait and see" attitude had clearly paid off.

After the first few weeks of classes, Eric collapsed on a chair in the living room of the house he shared with his parents. His mother was preparing dinner, and his father was working on a sermon he would give the following Sunday.

"Eric, you shouldn't be so hard on yourself. You've

only been back in China a month or so," James Liddell advised him.

"You don't know the latest news, Father. Now the school wants me to teach English, my worst subject. Besides, I've forgotten so much Chinese I can barely talk to my students anyway! How can I tell them about Jesus?" Eric sighed loudly.

"As I told you in Pei-tai-ho, the language you learned as a boy will return to you, but you must study every chance you get, son. And as for telling the boys about Jesus. . ."

Eric peered closely at the white-haired minister and missionary. "Yes, Father?"

"Remember your God-given talents, your running, your love of sports. They know nothing about you now—"

Smiling again, Eric slapped his leg excitedly. "I see what you mean! But, Father, that means—well, you know what they wear!"

All boys at the Anglo-Chinese College wore the school uniform—a floor-length, long-sleeved, dark blue cotton robe—for all school activities, including sports. That made learning any sport, especially those that involved running or kicking a ball, very difficult. Moreover, if there were even the slightest chance of rain, or if a player had been kicked accidentally in the shin, or if the team had little chance of winning, the Chinese students automatically refused to play.

But Eric knew he had a kindred spirit at the school in Dr. Hart. Long before Eric had arrived on the scene, Dr. Hart had espoused a "healthy minds in healthy bodies" philosophy. It was no secret that he couldn't have been more delighted to have an Olympic athlete on his staff. Years later, A. P. Cullen would write that sports "is one of the most productive fields for Christian work, for it remains generally true that the man who is a real sportsman in athletics, who can play the game under all circumstances, fight against odds and disappointments without losing heart or temper, and knows how to take a beating—he is the man who is most likely to be a true sportsman in the greater game of life."

So, feeling confident about his position, and after weeks of wondering what he should do, Eric took a drastic step. One day he stood before his students—in a tank top and shorts!

Running up and down the school's tiny grass field, Eric showed them how easy and fun sports could be. At first the boys laughed, but then they started rolling up their robes. It wasn't long before Eric made his case with the school directors to let the boys wear shorts for learning sports. When the decision was made, Eric became a very popular teacher.

As the boys' skills increased, Eric noticed another obvious need. The school had no real playing fields for games, and no stadium existed for athletic competition in the entire city of Tientsin. A few years later, under Eric's supervision, the Min Yuan Sports Field was completed, a sports arena modeled after London's Stamford Bridge stadium where Eric had run some of his greatest races.

His students were obviously drawn to him because of his sports skills and his ability to make anyone try their hardest on the playing fields. But Eric also made an impression at the school's morning worship services and at after-school Bible studies. Every morning, one teacher would speak to the entire school on the meaning of the day's scripture passage. The gift Eric had discovered years ago at Armadale in his first GSEU speech had not left him. Speaking simply, he touched the hearts of the boys and very quickly became their favorite speaker. And while many teachers shied away from including students in their family life, Eric regularly brought his boys home for what were known as "weekly Bible circles" or studies.

Oddly enough, Eric felt most uncomfortable in the classroom, where he was confined to standing rigidly in a suit, addressing the boys in a formal manner. Chemistry became his favorite subject, perhaps because of the laboratory sessions, where he would have more personal contact with the students. Over time, however, he became more at ease teaching all subjects.

Because the school was located in the French concession of Tientsin, an enclave populated by Westerners, the goings-on of the outside world often seemed surreal. But by Christmas 1925, a military conflict that had begun in western China was practically on Eric's doorstep. China's warlords, who had formerly controlled the provinces, were attempting in a last, gasping effort to wrest control of the country from the Kuomintang Party of Chiang Kai-shek and Mao Tse-tung.

When Siaochang, Eric's former home on the Great Plain, issued a desperate call for help for medical missionaries, Annie Buchan left immediately. By Christmas, the warlords had brought the battle to Tientsin, but their skirmishes were carefully orchestrated to avoid the Western enclaves. Many Chinese, however, lost their lives before the Kuomintang forces gained the upper hand. Unfortunately, two more years would pass before the northern warlords were completely subdued.

The crowning victory for Chiang Kai-shek occurred on June 4, 1928, when he captured Peking and proceeded to establish a new capital in the city of Nanking. This move by the Kuomintang Party signaled a new, unified leadership, one that, for a time, might offer new hope for the Christian missionaries. As Annie Buchan wrote at the end of 1928, "He [Chiang Kai-shek] was eager to see us advance in all aspects of our hospital work. Education was to have a higher standard; and. . .we saw the dawn of a new hope."

When the warlords had asserted themselves in the hinterland in May of 1928, the Siaochang mission hospital had been evacuated again. But, as Annie indicated, in the fall, "Dr. Rob," as he was known, and his family returned to Siaochang to supervise the rebuilding of the hospital and reestablish the mission compound.

Meanwhile in Tientsin, Eric's sports program for the students at the Anglo-Chinese College was in full swing. In the spring of 1926, he had organized the Annual College Sport track competition that would become a yearly and much-anticipated event. And in October 1928, he himself competed in the newly christened Far Eastern Games, conceived of by Japan's Emperor Hirohito as a way of making an impression on the world outside Asia. The games were held at the seaport of Port Arthur (today Lushun), which lies on the Liaotung Peninsula in northeast China. A huge stadium was constructed to host the event, and athletes from around the world arrived en masse.

These world-class athletes were fresh from the competition of the 1928 Amsterdam Olympic Games, an event Eric, by all accounts, could have participated in had he requested leave from the London Missionary Society. At Amsterdam, the 400-meter race had been won by Ray Barbuti, an American, with a time that was slower than Eric's Olympic-record pace. Fellow Brit Douglas Lowe had repeated as winner in the 800 meters.

At the Far Eastern Games, more than fifty thousand spectators crowded into the stands to witness Eric win the 200 meters with a time of 21.8 seconds, tying the winning time at Amsterdam set by Canada's Percy Williams. In the 400 meters, Eric again proved victorious, with a time of 47.8 seconds, tying Barbuti's time at Amsterdam. Without a training regimen, without the support of a national program, and without adequate facilities, Eric Liddell was still a world-class runner, still the best quarter-miler in the world.

As an exhibition event, Eric was chosen to run the 100 meters by himself. Sensing a unique photo opportunity, a Chinese photographer proceeded to place his tripod on the track at just the time Eric began to run, not realizing how fast Eric was coming or that he would be directly in his path. To the shrieks of the crowd, Eric stormed right into the photographer, sending the Chinese man and his tripod flying. Eric himself fell to the ground, flat on his face, and was knocked unconscious.

At that moment, two disheveled spectators began pushing their way through the crowd toward the fallen runner. Competently, they picked up Eric and carried him to a tent outside the track that had been designated for medical assistance. A few minutes later, when Eric came to, these two rather dusty and windblown vagabonds stared at him with bemused looks on their faces. Slightly confused at first and then overwhelmed, Eric started laughing in recognition. Annie and Rob were here in Manchuria—but how?

"Good race, old chap!" Rob greeted his brother, patting him on his arm as if nothing had happened. "We got here a little late, but we had no trouble picking you out of the pack, or for that matter, off the track!"

Annie nodded, trying to suppress a giggle. "Even the Chinese don't know what to make of you, Eric, and that includes photographers, I daresay. But I'll wager schoolboys will soon be opting for the windmill approach to running!"

The kidding went on until Eric held his hand up in surrender. "All right, you've had your fun. But how did you get here? Siaochang isn't exactly in the neighborhood."

Annie and Rob looked at each other and then nodded their heads. "A little visual aid is in order, I believe, but only if you're able to navigate," Rob said, grabbing Eric by the elbow and guiding him beyond the stadium. There, propped up against a wall, was the first motorcycle of the Siaochang mission compound and the transportation of choice on the notoriously dusty and bumpy roads of rural China.

"You came on this—to see me?" Eric shook his head in amazement.

"When you come from a family like ours that goes years between reunions and you find yourself in the same country—well, a very large country—and then you realize you've never seen an Olympic champion, who just so happens to be your brother, really run. . . ."

Such tributes always made Eric a little uncomfortable. For a moment, he stopped to think about his family and how treasured those years were in Siaochang, in Drymen, in Edinburgh, and now in Tientsin. Since he'd returned to China, he had lived with his parents for three years, and he hoped he hadn't taken that time for granted.

Another season of good-byes was inevitable, but Eric had no idea it would come upon him so suddenly.

TEN

Tientsin, China, 1929–35

In the summer of 1929, the London Missionary
Society informed James Liddell that he would
not be returning to the mission field following
his furlough. His health had been failing, and the
society did not want to put him at further risk in
the predictably unstable mission field of China.
But the thought of retirement after all his years of
service cast a pall over the Liddell home.

Eric had said good-bye to his parents and Jenny
and Ernest many times over the years, but on this
occasion he had never felt so alone.

As he faced his mother at the gangplank to the
German liner *Saarbrucken*, his voice cracked, and
he quickly wiped away a tear from his cheek. His
mother's face was wet with tears, too. "I will miss

you more than I can say," he whispered. His voice stopped as he buried his head in her shoulder.

"Eric, look at me. Perhaps now you can meet someone. . . ."

"She would have to be just like you, you know," he said, winking at her, his sense of humor surfacing again. "So don't hold your breath!"

Eric could joke with his mother, but in the months that followed, he missed their home life, even though he was enjoying the new apartment near the school that he shared with three other teachers and doctors. Years later, these men would all write memoirs of their experiences with Eric, remembering his sense of humor and unfailing kindness. As the surgeon George Dorling wrote, "We three were miles below the standard Eric set for himself. But he was always our friend. I knew that every time I could count on Eric. Nothing ever shocked him. His love was too great to be shocked."

On Sundays, he attended his father's church, where he had recently been appointed superintendent of the Sunday school. Before Sunday classes began, the children would gather for singing, led by Eric himself.

Eric arrived at Union Church earlier than usual one summer morning in 1929. He wanted to meet with the new organist to go over some songs he planned to teach the children. Hearing a door close at the end of the sanctuary, Eric turned around. A slender young woman, her short black curls bobbing up and down, was walking rapidly toward him.

"Hello, Eric," she said softly. "You don't remember me, do you?"

Eric couldn't help but smile at her shining face and mischievous dark flashing eyes. There was something familiar about her. "Has it been a few years?" he guessed.

"Oh, very good, yes, it has. And I was a young girl then, so you probably didn't notice me."

Eric laughed and rubbed his chin. "I can't imagine how I'd forget a face like yours. But I'd like to know where we met, Miss, er—"

"Florence Mackenzie. And it was Pei-tai-ho, the summer of 1925, right after you arrived from Scotland. I was only fourteen, but you still played games with me and my sister Margaret and, of course, all the other children there. Oh, and by the way, you were also my Sunday school teacher! Don't you remember the fun we had? Ah, well. We've just returned to Tientsin for another mission assignment, so here I am."

"Well, Miss Mackenzie, shall we begin?" Nervously Eric pointed to the music, not sure what to say.

Florence's parents had moved into a house not far from the Liddells' former home. And like Eric's parents, they enjoyed a house full of life, with people coming in and out, a house filled with laughter and singing. Eric felt immediately at home there, even though his thoughts about Florence were far from comforting. Florence, on the other hand, had loved Eric from the time she first met him years before, but she had told no one. Her heart beat faster when she caught Eric staring at her, or when he touched her arm to get her attention.

No one suspected that Eric and Florence were "courting," least of all Florence herself. At age seventeen, Florence was certainly not allowed to be alone with a man of twenty-seven, even if he were the esteemed Eric Liddell. So whenever they were together, they were always in a large group.

A late summer camping trip, organized by several missionary families, might have provided a clue as to Eric's feelings, but only to the more astute. As the group of ten began ascending Mount Pei-Niu-Ting, the home of a famous Chinese hermit, Eric carried most of Florence's supplies and offered to help her in any way he could. When the group decided to take a rest after hours of arduous climbing, Eric was nowhere to be found. Then someone pointed to the summit, high above them.

"It's Eric, but how did he get up there so fast?"

Another woman, the wife of a missionary, replied knowingly, "That's Eric's idea of a rest!"

To others, it might have appeared that Eric was trying to show off. But this man of God only wanted time alone with his heavenly Father. Only

God knew that Eric had fallen in love. As soon as he returned from the camping trip, Eric sent a telegram to his mother and Jenny with a very particular request. Being shy about matters of the heart, Eric had decided he would wait until his requested parcel from them arrived before declaring his feelings—but love stories aren't written so predictably.

When Florence began her senior year of high school that fall of 1929, her eyes were firmly fastened on one goal. At the end of the academic year, she and Margaret would set sail for Toronto—she to enter nursing school, and her sister to begin at the university. But those plans were in jeopardy when Florence discovered she had failed her French exam.

"Eric, I don't know what I'll do. The nursing school will never accept me now, not with such a mark on my record!" Eric had come to her parents' home for one of his usual visits, but the sight of Florence's tearstained face was more than he could bear. She was usually so bubbly, so vivacious, so encouraging! He had, of course, counseled downcast students, but never before the one woman he loved with all his heart.

"You mustn't for one moment think of giving up. Florence, you must promise me you won't!" Eric's blue eyes held hers for several seconds, until she nodded feebly. "Now, you're not going to sit here another minute feeling sorry for yourself.

Come on, Flossie, let's go for a walk."

Eric always called her Flossie when he was teasing her, so Florence wrinkled up her nose. "Well, if you put it like that, all right. Let me just grab a sweater." With a new bounce in her step, she joined Eric a few minutes later and they proceeded to stroll down the street—alone together.

Several blocks later, he stopped laughing and suddenly gathered both her hands into his. "There's something I've been wanting to ask you for such a long time. And I can't think of a better time than this, though it may be years—"

"Yes, Eric?" Florence interrupted his rambling sentence, her eyes now clear and shining.

"Will you marry me, Florence Mackenzie?" he whispered.

Florence threw her arms around his neck and held him close. "I thought you'd never ask!" she whispered breathlessly. Cupping his hands around her face, Eric kissed her gently on the lips.

A few months later, the long-awaited package arrived. As Florence opened the jeweler's box, lovingly wrapped by Eric's mother and sister, she cried in delight at the lovely five-stone diamond engagement ring.

"This is just like the ring my father gave my mother," Eric said, slipping it on her finger. "Because you are the only woman I want to share my life with," he added. Florence and Eric could finally share their happy news with family and friends.

In the summer of 1930, Florence left for Toronto with her sister, as planned. Eric's confidence in her, not to mention the joy she felt over her engagement, had boosted her grades, and she had been accepted into nursing school at Toronto General Hospital. A year later, Eric himself left Tientsin for his first furlough as a missionary. On his way to Scotland, he stopped first in Canada to see the Mackenzies, who were almost as delighted about the upcoming marriage as Eric and Florence.

But marriage was clearly far into the future. Like James and Mary Liddell, Eric and Florence were resigned to a very long engagement.

On August 31, 1931, Waverley Station was the scene of another raucous celebration. Six years had passed since most of Edinburgh had waved farewell to their illustrious native son, and now they would welcome him back in similar fashion. Eric Liddell had left, but he was hardly forgotten.

While the press had been quite clear about the purpose of Eric's furlough, invitations arrived daily at the Scottish Congregational College, where he was enrolled for the next two terms to finish his ordination training. In fact, the demand to see him was so great that a college committee was set up with the sole purpose of coordinating his appearance schedule!

For the following year, he would be booked every Sunday as the guest speaker in churches throughout England, Ireland, and Scotland. D. P. Thomson and other alumni of the GSEU made sure he made all the rounds in Scotland, and Elsa McKechnie and members of the still-thriving Eric Liddell Fan Club wanted time with their hero as well. Eric's parents were only too glad he was staying with them, and they accepted calmly the demands on their son. Their family was growing up and leaving them—Ernest had entered business college in Edinburgh and Jenny was engaged and planning a spring wedding—so they welcomed any time they could spend with their children.

At a "Welcome Home Meeting" in Edinburgh, a rally attended by leading church officials and members of the sports community, Eric's speech conveyed eloquently his new purpose in life:

> We are all missionaries. We carry our
> religion with us, or we allow our religion to
> carry us. Wherever we go, we either bring
> people nearer to Christ, or we repel them from
> Christ. We are working for the great kingdom
> of God—the time when all people will turn to
> Christ as their Leader—and will not be afraid
> to own Him as such.

And while Eric touched briefly on the political

situation in China, he wanted much more simply to share God's love. Whenever he was asked for his autograph, he obliged, adding several Chinese characters as well, symbols that were so revealing of the man. The characters meant, "Keep smiling." He was still the Olympic champion who had made it his habit to greet his competitors before a race. The setting was different, but the stakes had never been higher.

Indeed, those same Chinese characters would lead to a life-changing encounter while Eric was on furlough. When Eric told a friend what the characters meant, the friend immediately said, "There's a woman I know I think you should meet. One of her favorite sayings is 'Keep smiling'—but with her it's incredible she can even say that."

The friend went on to tell Eric about Bella, who five years earlier had been involved in a horrendous accident. She had lost one eye, had much of her scalp removed, and was in danger of losing sight in the remaining eye. After undergoing numerous skin grafts, Bella still suffered mind-numbing headaches and now was told she would probably go deaf. Every month she had to return to the hospital to have eyelashes pulled from the lid of her working eye, as they were growing inward and damaging the eye. Still, she clung to her faith in God, and thus could say without reservation, "Keep smiling." Upon hearing her story, Eric wanted to meet her if at all possible.

During the hour he spent with Bella, she held his hand the entire time. She revealed that she, too, worked for the Lord and that she was a great admirer of his. And then she told him something he would never forget. "There are people in this world who suffer much more than I, you know. My sufferings are nothing compared with theirs. So when I hear someone complain about trivial things, I tell them my story to show how fortunate they really are."

The next day, just before Eric boarded a train for London, he received a letter from Bella, saying how pleased she was that he could visit her. The letter had arrived, as all things from God, just in time. Sitting across from Eric on the train was a young man who was visibly distraught. In no time, with a little encouragement from Eric, the man began unraveling his woeful tale.

His life was in shambles. Nothing had ever worked out for him, and now he couldn't keep a job or his girlfriend. "There's nothing left for me but to kill myself," he said, concluding the sad litany. And then he put his head in his hands.

Eric did not want to point out the errors of the young man's ways, as that was not his style. Instead, he chose to befriend him, and he would do so with Bella's letter. Drawing the letter from his pocket, he said to the downcast passenger, "Just read it once. Please."

Bella's note had, of course, ended with those familiar words, "Keep smiling." But there was nothing unusual about her note. The young man looked confused and shook his head. Then Eric told him Bella's story, not leaving out a single detail.

Almost at once, the man's face brightened and he admitted that, yes, he had lost faith in God and himself. Bella's letter, like her ministry, had given him hope to go on and to seek God's answers for his life. When he got off in London, he was not the same man who had boarded the train in Edinburgh.

If my furlough ended right now, Eric thought, *I would consider myself blessed.* But there were other exciting events yet to occur. Jenny's wedding to Dr. Charles Somerville would be one of those rare occasions that brought all the Liddells together. Rob and his wife and family traveled all the way from Siaochang for the happy occasion but quickly returned to their home.

Two months later, on June 22, 1932, most of the Liddell family gathered for another celebration when Eric Henry Liddell was formally ordained at the Scottish Congregational College.

The happy event also brought another reason to say good-bye. With his ordination, the Reverend Eric Liddell's first furlough had come to an end. He needed to be back at Tientsin in September for the start of the fall term, and he needed to be in Canada to see Florence before that. In the last two years, they had spent only a few weeks together, even though they had corresponded regularly. Once again, Waverley Station would be the scene of an emotional farewell, but this time a very personal one.

After embracing her son, Mary placed her roughened hands lovingly around his face. "Out in China, we so dreaded the long good-byes—as maybe you now know. So as not to cry, we missionaries decided to make them more joyful."

Will I never stop learning from her? Eric thought. "And how did you do that, Mother?" He couldn't help smiling at her sweet face.

"We always said, those who love God never meet for the last time. That made it a meeting, not a parting, don't you see?"

Still he clung to her again and then reached for his father one last time. He would remember his mother's words.

Eric's reunion with Florence was as joyous as he had hoped, and the Mackenzies made him feel as welcome as he had in Scotland. While in Toronto, word of his visit leaked out to the British Olympic track team, which was training there before leaving for the 1932 Summer Olympics in Los Angeles. Eric was only too happy to meet with them, and at the time he also consented to be interviewed. When asked by R. E. Knowles, who was covering the Olympic team, whether he had any regrets about leaving the limelight, Eric offered a balanced answer. "Oh, well, of course," he began offhandedly, "it's natural for a chap to think over all that sometimes, but I'm glad I'm at the work I'm engaged in now. A fellow's life counts for far more at this than the other." Pausing a moment, he then referred to Paul's letter to the church at Corinth, adding, "Not a corruptible crown, but an incorruptible, you know!"

As Eric set sail for China, he traveled with a sense of confidence that he knew what awaited him. He would resume his duties at the Anglo-Chinese College and at his church—and in those rare moments when he allowed himself to daydream, he would envision the day he would again meet Florence. But that next time, coming down the aisle of Union Church, she would be his bride.

Eric returned to a China again engulfed in conflict, but it was hardly unexpected. For years, the Nationalist wing of the Kuomintang Party had been at odds with the Chinese Communist Party of Mao Tse-tung. Now that Chiang Kai-shek had established a unified government in Nanking, he sought to control the political soul of China, as well—and that meant launching a new series of campaigns against the Communists.

Meanwhile, Japan had made her move against China, seizing Manchuria in 1931 and gradually applying increasing pressure in the north. By 1932, Japan had launched a savage attack against Shanghai, flattening much of the city, which was then the largest seaport in the Far East. Tientsin was miraculously spared, but for Eric, that did not mean business as usual.

Since Dr. Hart's retirement in 1930, which signaled, along with the Liddells' departure, the end of a missionary generation, the Anglo-Chinese College had been in a state of confusion. Dr. Hart had planned that his successor be Chinese to ensure that the school one day would be administered entirely by a non-Western missionary board. However, not one successor, but several, had followed during the next two years, the result of tense relations between the Chinese administrator and his staff.

For that reason, upon Eric's return from furlough, he was assigned many new duties, some of which had been the province of Dr. Hart. He would now serve as the college secretary, handling correspondence and keeping records of all students and faculty, act as chairman of the games committee, and be in charge of all religious activities of the college. If that weren't enough, in his spare time, Eric decided to try his hand at journalism. To inspire future missionaries, he would pen his own column in the London Missionary Society magazine. When he was at Eltham, he remembered reading similar columns in the magazine and recognized how those articles had cemented his desire to follow his parents into the mission field.

Perhaps another reason Eric threw himself headlong into all these responsibilities was to make the year pass more quickly without Florence—and indeed, by the fall of 1933, it seemed he had almost succeeded.

He was sitting in Union Church one Sunday, having just read the scripture passage, "Lo, I am with you alway," when he sensed the presence of his father with him. He hadn't seen his father, but he seemed to feel he was there beside him. The next morning, Eric received a cablegram informing him that James Liddell had died peacefully the day before, sitting in his favorite chair in Drymen, Scotland.

Overcome with grief, Eric wondered about the Lord's purpose in such a situation. Why had God waited to bring James home to heaven after Eric had returned to China? Now Eric was thousands of miles away, unable to return home for the funeral or to comfort his family. A few weeks later, Eric received a letter from his father, written shortly before his death. James simply wanted to wish Eric the best with his work and his marriage. The message was clear to Eric: He was meant to be right where he was and to do God's work, just as his father had done for more than thirty years.

On the same day that Eric received his father's last letter, November 27, 1933, Florence passed her final nursing exams in Toronto. Two months later, preceded by her father, she and her mother left for China. And five weeks after setting sail from Vancouver on the *Empress of Canada*, they were hovering outside the harbor of Tientsin. Confounded by a strong offshore wind that had caused the water level to drop dramatically, the ship could not enter the harbor to dock. The boat needed a fifteen-foot water clearance to enter the mouth of the river, and then into the harbor. All the time that the ship waited, she was being battered from gale-force winds. How much longer could the ship withstand such an assault? From the shore, Eric and his future father-in-law, Hugh Mackenzie, watched the ocean liner anxiously, desperately trying to get information about the ship's status. Finally, the word was given: The harbormaster had decided to take the risk with a thirteen-foot clearance and bring the ship in.

When Eric and Florence were reunited after many long hours, the couple talked well into the night, eagerly making plans, and at the same time catching up on each other's news. The Anglo-Chinese College was to have a short break at the end of March, so Eric and Florence decided to schedule their wedding for that weekend. It was time for their four-year engagement to come to a close!

On March 27, 1934, Eric and Florence were married in Union Church, an event that merited front-page coverage in the *Peking and Tientsin Times* and *North China News*:

There was a large attendance of foreigners and Chinese at the Union Church this afternoon when the Reverend Eric H. Liddell, the well-known Olympic champion, was united in matrimony with Miss Florence Jean MacKenzie, the daughter of Mr. and Mrs. Hugh MacKenzie, well-known and much-respected residents of Tientsin. Prior to this, the civil ceremony took place this morning at the HBM Consulate before M.S.G. Beare, HBM Consul.

The nuptial knot was tied by Rev. Eric Richards (minister of Union Church) assisted by Dr. Murdoch MacKenzie, who, besides having been a resident in China for the past forty-three years, also christened the bride. To the strains of Lohengrin's "Wedding March," the bride entered on the arm of her father, who gave her away.

The bride's wedding dress, which was also her mother's wedding dress, was of white satin with lace veil trimmed with a sprig of orange blossoms, and she carried a bouquet of pink carnations. The lace veil had also been worn by Miss Liddell, the sister of the bridegroom, at her own wedding. . . . Mrs. Hugh MacKenzie, the bride's mother, wore a black georgette dress, trimmed with lace, with black hat to match, and she carried a bouquet of pink carnations. The church was artistically decorated for the occasion with flowers and plants. . . .

After the religious ceremony, a reception was held at the home of the bride's parents, No. 70 Cambridge Road, and was attended by a large number of the many friends of the happy couple. The guests were received under a large silver bell covered with ferns and pink carnations.

One year and a few months later, Eric and Florence were the parents of a little girl, whom they named Patricia. As he gazed into the blue eyes of his rambunctious daughter, Eric felt hope and also anxiety. In the year since he had married, so much had happened to him and to his world. He had once been so sure of his position at the Anglo-Chinese College, so sure of his students, so sure of his goals.

The words to his favorite hymn, "Finlandia," came to him in moments like this: "Be still, my soul, the Lord is on thy side."

ELEVEN

From Tientsin to Siaochang, 1935–39

Civil war had erupted in the early 1930s between the Nationalists and Communists. Mao Tsetung, ever the champion of China's peasant population, had joined forces with the former warlord Zhu De and with Zhou Enlai and was employing guerrilla tactics to draw the Nationalists into unfamiliar rural terrain. There the Nationalists, still under the direction of Chiang Kai-shek, began to suffer tremendous losses as they were slowly being destroyed by Mao's Red Army.

However, Chiang could not be counted out. In 1934, he led a last-ditch effort to counter Mao's tactics by throwing a blockade around the Communist bases. Bursting through the blockade, the Red Army then began what has become known as the Long March, trooping six thousand miles northwest to Shaanxi Province where they would establish new bases.

Only a conflict of greater magnitude could bring two such opposed military forces together. And only an enemy like Japan could make two stubborn leaders agree to work as one—for the time being. Since Japan had invaded Manchuria in 1931, she had not ceased in her pursuit of other provinces, and such forays had only been aided and abetted by the ongoing civil war. In 1935, Japan even penetrated the Great Wall north of Peking. There was no real resistance to the Japanese until 1937, when a minor incident at Peking's Marco Polo Bridge marked the beginning of outright war. A month later, Mao and Chiang were reluctant bedfellows, engaged in the same guerrilla tactics that had once distinguished the Red Army. Together, they formed a united front against their archenemy.

The main body of the Red Army was reorganized into what would be known as the Eighth Route Army of the National Revolutionary Army, an army that would become well known to the dwellers in Siaochang. Siaochang, the rural, backward mission compound of Eric's youth and now home to Annie Buchan and "Dr. Rob," was a strategic position. Two main railway routes, from Tientsin to Shanghai, and from Peking to Hankow, passed within forty miles to the east and fifty miles to the west of Siaochang. All too soon, the railways would be controlled by the Japanese, but the land in between—in other words, Siaochang—would be the domain of the Chinese. And a certain mission compound might mean the difference between life and death.

The summer of 1935 found Eric and Florence at Pei-tai-ho, along with the wives and children of other Western missionaries. Eric wasn't supposed to be taking his vacation so early, but he needed time to think and to be alone with Flo. Their first child was due in a month, and they needed to make a major decision before then.

Earlier in the year, Eric had received word from the district council of the London Missionary Society that their rural mission stations in China were seriously understaffed. As a teacher at the Anglo-Chinese College, where it was rumored too many Society missionaries held positions, he was asked to consider assuming a position at Siaochang.

"Flo, you don't know what Siaochang is like, and with a baby coming—"

"I know what it's like, Eric. You forget that I read Annie's and Rob's letters, too. There is a miserable drought, not to mention all the soldiers and the fighting. But that's not all, is it?"

Eric shook his head despondently. A missionary wasn't supposed to get used to the good life, the life they enjoyed in Tientsin. He had a dream job, surrounded by highly intelligent students and colleagues, and a home life that was almost idyllic, in a safe and protected compound with an adoring wife and a baby soon to join them. There was always the threat of war, even in Tientsin, and lately Eric had been forced to conduct compulsory military drills with his students. To counter that, he had organized a voluntary breakfast prayer group among the faculty to pray for peace in China. But to give all this up. . .for Siaochang?

Before he had left for their summer retreat, Eric had been barraged with pleas from the missionaries in Tientsin not to leave. They couldn't understand why he would even consider "throwing away" his bachelor of science degree and his years of teaching experience to become a rural pastor.

"There's only one course to follow, Flo," Eric finally said. "I've got to pray, and then pray some more. In time, God will show me His will."

At summer's end, Eric sent this cablegram to the London Missionary Society:

> *The summer brought me face-to-face with the question as to whether I felt called to country work, seeing that that section of the work was so understaffed. I thought over it then, and have been thinking over it ever since, and cannot but feel that I am more equipped for educational work, both by training and temperament.*

Besides, at the present time it would make it extremely difficult in the college to reduce numbers.

Eric's decision hadn't dampened his brother's enthusiastic correspondence, as throughout the fall of 1935 and the early months of 1936 Rob continued to urge him to come to Siaochang. The London Missionary Society was likewise undeterred. By July, the society had decided that Eric should be released from the college for four months to pursue rural missionary work, and Eric was resigned to go.

He and Flo spent another summer respite at Pei-tai-ho, this time watching one-year-old Patricia take her first steps. His letters to his mother were full of her granddaughter's achievements and the hope that she would be able to meet her grandchildren soon. Flo was three months' pregnant with their second child, and Eric's furlough wouldn't be for another three years.

In September Eric left for his trial stay in Siaochang, alone. Florence and Patricia would remain in Tientsin, but they would never be far from his thoughts.

As he made his way to Siaochang, the old mule cart in which he was a passenger managed to sink its wheels in every pothole along the dusty country road. Bouncing up and down in the passenger seat, Eric felt his legs and arms ache. He longed to get out and stretch his body. He longed to be back in Tientsin.

As expected, signs of the drought and the military presence were everywhere. And what hadn't been destroyed by man had been eaten by locusts. People were starving to death because nothing would grow on their farms, and people were killing each other for food. Hunger and disease were rampant.

As the mud gates of Siaochang came into view, Eric thought about himself. *I'm not a village pastor. I'm a teacher. Just because I lived here doesn't mean I'll know how to help these people. Why, God, why am I here?*

Before he had left Tientsin, Florence had answered that question for him. She had never known Eric as the Olympic champion, but she did know her husband. "Eric, you knew it was wrong to run on Sunday, and you know it's wrong not to go where God has called you. You have no choice but to go."

And then Eric noticed the sign over the gates, the one placed there shortly after the Boxer Rebellion, the one that had meant so much to his mother decades earlier. Although the paint was peeling, the characters were still legible: *Chung Wai, I Chai*—Chinese and Foreigners, All One Home. Eric couldn't help but question the truth of that statement.

But even though almost thirty years had passed, the people of Siaochang still remembered Eric, and they remembered the wonderful work of his parents. "Thank you for coming, Li Mu Shi!" they cried as they circled him. Li Mu Shi was the name they had given his father all those years ago—"Li," short for Liddell, and "Mu Shi," a name that means Pastor.

"I'm glad you're here, too," a familiar voice exclaimed behind him.

"And I hope you haven't forgotten that I work here, too!" chimed in Annie Buchan. "All our letters and mostly our prayers—and here you are at last."

Turning, Eric gave his brother Rob a big hug and put his arm around Annie, as well. He had left his family, but he was not alone. To his surprise, his feelings of despair soon vanished, and his heart was filled with joy. Yes, he was needed here, and yes, he was home.

Later, Florence would write to D. P. Thomson of Eric's change of heart:

> After much prayerful consideration of all the points involved, he felt God was calling him to the country, and I think it was quite obvious he did the right thing. He loved the work, his health improved, and I think he blossomed out in a new way.

When Eric returned to Tientsin, he had made his decision. Following their family's summer stay in Pei-tai-ho, a family that now included baby Heather, he would assume the position of a rural missionary, working out of Siaochang. Florence and the two children would continue living in the French enclave in Tientsin, a location still deemed secure.

Rather than dwell on all he was leaving behind, Eric began to focus on what was ahead. He would be assisting his brother and a few other missionaries at the hospital, offering rudimentary care to those in the overcrowded facility. And as pastor, he would be following in his father's footsteps. Already he had seen how large those footprints were, and how puny his efforts might be.

And he was also following in his Father's steps. To bring hope where there was none, to share a smile and a laugh, and to impart in his inadequate Chinese the love of God—yes, that was God's will for Eric Liddell.

He had come full circle.

The year after Eric left the Anglo-Chinese College permanently for the mission compound of Siaochang, the college's annual report carried this tribute: "To say that we have missed him, not only in his Science teaching and in Athletics. . .would be to say the least that is possible." Indeed, in the spring of 1937, two events occurred that would not only underscore the annual report, but would also provide closure to Eric's thirteen years in Tientsin.

First, the North China track championships were held at the Min Yuan Sports Field, the complex that Eric had lovingly supervised from its inception. To see "his boys" competing in such an arena was all the tribute Eric needed. More importantly, though, before he left the college, forty-nine boys were baptized, including a few of the more incorrigible ones whose hearts had been hardened to spiritual matters.

Eric arrived at Siaochang before Christmas, but the scene that greeted him was far from festive. It was a place full of misery and fear. Despite the evangelistic efforts of missionaries, most of the rural people still worshiped several gods, including the kitchen god. Once a year, on the Chinese New Year, the picture of last year's god was burned, but not until sugar had been rubbed on its mouth so that it would say only good things about its owner in the next life.

Tens of thousands of people lived in the tiny villages on the Great Plain, villages that had been terrorized by bandits, Japanese soldiers, Chinese guerrilla fighters, and drought. Many of the homes Eric remembered had been destroyed, and it was common for several families to share one humble dwelling.

The area that Eric would be serving was roughly the size of Wales. He would be based at Siaochang, but his duties would be those of an itinerant preacher, traveling from village to village across the Great Plain on foot or by bicycle, enduring extremes of bitter cold and scorching heat. Wherever he went, the sounds of exploding shells and machine guns could be heard in the distance—or at close range. Often he arrived at a village only to find the charred remains of homes, large numbers of dead bodies, and survivors who were numb with shock.

To solve his language problem, Eric traveled with an interpreter named Wang Feng Chou. Before he and Wang entered a village, they would sometimes be asked to recognize one or two Chinese characters written on a blackboard. Only those who lived on the Plain would know what they meant and could then enter. Wang was also astute at recognizing the signs of Japanese occupation, and he and Eric would then change their route for the day. Through Wang, Eric convinced many older village men to cut their queues, their traditional pigtails, for protection. One form of Japanese torture involved hanging men by their queues. There were no young men in the villages as all those under the age of forty-five had been sent to fight in the Nationalist Army.

Eric had little to give the villagers except a message of hope, a message from God's Word, and of course, his infectious, disarming smile. In fact, his smile became his passport along the country roads and at village gates where he would often be searched for weapons by both Chinese guerrilla fighters and Japanese soldiers. Eric would politely endure all frisking and then flash his inimitable smile—and his captors would always let him pass on his way.

But danger was everywhere, and the fighting continued day in and day out. Once, several missionaries gathered together to hold a baptismal service for the villages near Siaochang. Heavy gunfire could be heard on Saturday night, and by Sunday morning enemy planes were circling overhead. An attack was imminent.

As Eric began conducting the Sunday service, shells began exploding just outside the village church. Seemingly unflappable, Eric kept on going. Then a fleet of trucks tore into the village, and the footfalls of soldiers could be heard searching all the buildings. Instead of giving in to his fear, Eric started singing, and soon those present joined in, too. When the soldiers entered the church, they simply looked around and left.

At the end of the service, those people who lived in the village raced outside to their homes, suspecting the worst. But the Japanese soldiers had been shooting at bandits and were not interested in robbing the people or harming their village. Only the effects of the shelling were evident; they hadn't vandalized the property.

That night, no villagers turned up for the evening service, but Eric and the missionaries were still there. They had decided to leave for their homes at dawn. Suddenly, a sound outside made them jump and then the door to the church slowly opened. Holding a lantern in his hand was the local opium addict, who fell to his knees in front of the missionaries.

Everyone thought this man was in prison. He had been arrested and tried, but then miraculously set free. During his trial he had prayed to God for his salvation and he had been acquitted. The former addict had just returned to the village and was unaware of the bombing earlier in the day. He was so excited about his freedom and his newfound faith that he simply had to find a church service to attend.

Now that Eric had a "congregation" to preach to, the evening service went on as scheduled.

But there were also failures, when all Eric could do was stand by helplessly. He and Wang once entered a village and were about to approach an old man, sitting outside his house. The man had refused to answer a Japanese soldier's questions, and the soldier was searching his house. When the soldier came outside, he accosted the old man and then shot him in the face in front of Eric and Wang. Later at the mission hospital, his face contorted with grief, Eric said to Annie, "I just stood there. And then I thought, what would God have done?"

As the summer of 1938 approached, Rob and his wife and daughter were due to take their furlough. "Dr. Rob" had served many years without leave and recently he himself had been quite ill. Annie would stay on, but the hospital would be without a highly trained physician. Though he was hardly a substitute, Eric learned first aid and took on Rob's duties as well, despite claiming that he only knew how to administer iodine.

After a short break at Pei-tai-ho with his family, whom he hadn't seen for eight months, Eric returned to Siao-chang. As he began to put his own stamp on the Siaochang compound, the mission hospital came to be known as a rescue station. Eric wouldn't turn away anyone: Japanese or Chinese, enemy soldier, guerrilla fighter, or bandit. When asked how he could do this, Eric answered, "They [the patients] are neither Japanese nor Chinese, soldier nor civilian. They are all men Christ died for." Along with providing medical care, Eric had in mind administering spiritual lessons as well. Whenever a nearby village was badly shelled, hundreds of refugees would invariably seek temporary shelter at the mission—where they discovered much more than needed protection.

At the same time, Annie Buchan was instrumental in establishing a baby clinic in an effort to combat the ever-increasing infant mortality rate. The stresses of everyday life had caused many mothers to be unable to nurse their babies, and those infants were starving to death. A soya-bean milk kitchen was started, where milk was made from crushed soya beans mixed with calcium and sugar. This concoction proved inexpensive and effective in saving many lives.

But despite the missionaries' efforts, the Siaochang mission was in danger of closing. By early 1939, the Japanese flag hung over the entrance to the mission, in an effort to scare people away. That it did, but the unfurled symbol of the enemy did not intimidate the missionaries. Shortly after the flag was hung, Annie Buchan left Siaochang for a much-needed rest. When she returned a month later, much to her astonishment, a Scottish flag hung over the mission—but only for a few hours. The Japanese were not pleased with the prank and demanded an explanation. Only after Eric explained that it was "a joke on an honorable matron" did the Japanese decide to forget the matter.

Clearly, the Japanese wanted missionaries like Eric out of Siaochang because they prevented them from assuming complete control of the area. But that didn't deter Eric from carrying out his responsibilities.

Whenever the mission ran short of coal, someone would have to make the four-hundred-mile trek to Tientsin for the money to purchase the coal, and then travel on to Tehchow to have the coal placed on barges for delivery to Siaochang. Although the journey was arduous, Eric didn't mind because it gave him another opportunity to see Flo and the children, who were still living in Tientsin. On this particular trip in the winter of 1939, Eric accomplished the first leg, to Tientsin, without any difficulty and stayed two days. But when he reached Tehchow, bandits stole half the coal. Farther along, another group of bandits stole the rest. Eric returned to Tientsin for more money.

Hiding the money in a hollowed-out loaf of bread, Eric then boarded a train for Tehchow. But guerrillas sabotaged the transport and Eric and the rest of the passengers had to wait twenty-four hours in the bitter cold of winter for another train. Eventually, he reached Tehchow and then Siaochang with the coal intact, but he was completely exhausted. At the mission hospital he was greeted with the last news he wanted to hear: They were running dangerously low on medical supplies. Two days later, Eric set off for Tientsin again, this time by mule cart.

When he reached an inn to spend the night, he was informed that a wounded Chinese soldier was nearby, lying in an abandoned temple. He had been there for five days, but the villagers were afraid to go near him because of reprisals from the Japanese. This was an understandable reaction given the notoriously harsh treatment administered by the Japanese whenever Chinese guerrillas had encroached on territory controlled by the Japanese. Usually the Japanese would burn the villagers' homes or behead randomly selected adults.

Even though he was afraid, Eric knew he had been placed in this situation so that he could somehow rescue this poor soldier. Accompanied by the mule carter, who only agreed to go because he felt he would be safe with a "man of God," Eric made his way to the filthy, rat-infested temple. Some villagers had managed to sneak in rags for the soldier to lie on, but Eric knew the man could not last much longer in his present state. Eric promised to return for the soldier the next morning. He would have the night to consider the best course of action.

That night Eric was on his knees for much of the time, seeking God's guidance. What would he say if a Japanese soldier stopped him? The soldier would have to notice the wounded Chinese soldier—and then Eric might put an entire village at risk. Was saving one man worth endangering many more people? Pulling out his Bible from his satchel, he turned to Luke 16:10: "He that is faithful in that which is least is faithful also in much; and he that is unjust in the least is unjust also in much." Eric knew exactly what God was telling him to do.

The next morning, just as Eric and the mule carter were again nearing the abandoned temple, they noticed a man they didn't know near the village gates, waving them to go away. As soon as Eric and the carter had found a safe shelter, they realized the danger they had been in. In a few minutes, Japanese troops began passing by, a convoy that would have been sure to question Eric and the carter.

When the soldiers were gone, Eric and the carter helped the wounded soldier into the mule cart, and they started on their way back to Siaochang. The hospital would have to make do without the supplies for a few more days. But Eric's adventure wasn't over yet.

On their way, a farmer informed them that another wounded man was lying in a shed nearby, in desperate need of medical help. When they reached him, they noticed his neck was heavily bound with blood-soaked rags. This peasant man had been dragged from his home, along with five others, to be questioned and then executed. The farmer told Eric that the others had knelt down submissively to be executed, but this man had refused to comply. In anger, a Japanese soldier had slashed at his neck, and the man had fallen down, appearing mortally wounded. After the Japanese left the area, the villagers had discovered that this man was still alive, although his head was almost severed from his body.

Eric and the carter carefully lifted the peasant man onto the cart as well. As they continued on their eighteen-mile journey back to Siaochang, enemy planes circled overhead. A mile away, the sounds of shelling reverberated in the air and the ground shook. Despite the ever-present danger, God was with them. They reached Siaochang, and the two men received medical attention.

Sadly, the wounded Chinese soldier died two days later, but the peasant man survived. And Eric, after a rest, made an uneventful trip to Tientsin for the hospital supplies. *Danger is everywhere,* Eric thought, *but so are miracles.*

(Later Eric would learn that the man whose life he had saved—the peasant man who had refused to be killed—was a gifted artist named Li Hsin Sheng. Li's painting of a peony, which the artist gave to Eric, still graces many homes around the world. Eric had liked the painting so much that he had it made into lithographs to give as gifts to friends, among them Elsa McKechnie, on the occasion of her marriage.)

In the summer of 1939, Eric met his family again in Tientsin to prepare to leave on furlough. It was not easy leaving the mission compound. The situation in Siaochang was extremely precarious, and Eric feared what he would find upon his return. But for the time being, he was glad to be leaving Tientsin. The Japanese were now in control of this strategic port city, including railways, the postal service, and the newspapers. To finance their war effort, the Japanese had flooded Tientsin with heroin for sale, as well as inexpensive Japanese goods.

Eric heaved a sigh of relief when he and his family were safely on board a ship bound across the Pacific. They would sail to Hawaii and then Vancouver, before taking the train to Toronto. China was no place for his little girls.

TWELVE

From Siaochang to Tientsin, 1939–41

Later in the summer, Eric sailed alone from Canada to Scotland. Florence and the children were happily ensconced in Toronto with the Mackenzies—who were delighted to meet their grandchildren for the first time—and Eric had much to attend to back home. Besides, a world war was imminent, with all that implied, and he didn't want his family to be in unnecessary danger. Nor did he want to be left behind.

While Eric and Florence had been planning their furlough earlier that year, Adolf Hitler had planned his onslaught of Poland. As the Liddells landed on Canadian soil, Josef Stalin of Russia signed a nonaggression pact with Hitler over Poland, which was immediately followed by Hitler's invasion of the beleaguered Eastern European country. As Eric was preparing to leave for Scotland, Britain and France had no choice but to declare war on Germany on September 3, 1939, signaling the start of World War II.

After spending Christmas with his mother, Jenny and Charles, and Ernest, who was now training to be a lieutenant in the Royal Artillery (following Rob, who had already enlisted), Eric decided to write and volunteer his own services to the war effort. He had envisioned a distinct role for himself, one typical of his heroic sports career and adventurous spirit as a missionary in China. He wanted nothing less than to be a fighter pilot in the Royal Air Force.

The RAF wrote him back, but not with the news he wanted to hear. They could offer him a desk job, but at his age, he was too old to assume command of a warplane. Thirty-seven-year-old Eric was still as fit as he had been several years earlier. Although friends in Scotland thought he had aged more than they expected, the months spent in Siaochang bicycling to distant villages had given him a lean, muscular appearance. In response to the RAF's offer, Eric wrote, "If you're only going to stick me behind a desk, then I've got more important work to do."

Florence and the girls joined him in Edinburgh in March 1940 for a delightful five-month visit with Mary Liddell, who thoroughly enjoyed her first opportunity to get to know her granddaughters Patricia and Heather. When it was time for the Liddell family to leave England for Canada, they knew it would not be a simple undertaking. Britain was at war, and this voyage would be full of reminders of that fact.

Eric, Florence, and the girls would be sailing on a small steamer that was part of a convoy of fifty ships. But just off the Irish coast, the very ship they were on was struck by a torpedo—a torpedo that failed to explode. Another ship in their convoy was struck and later sank, and the remaining vessels went into a defensive zigzag formation. The ships sailed at high speed for the next three days to avoid the enemy.

On Sunday, Eric was asked to preside over the ship's morning service. Aware that he was hardly dressed for the role of minister, he began, "I hope you won't mind that I'm in my sports coat and flannels!" The passengers and crew, tense from the recent emergency, were glad for the chance to laugh. Then Eric proceeded to talk about what it means to be truly thankful.

When their ship finally reached Nova Scotia, they were startled to learn that the German government had declared the waters around Britain to be a "sphere of intensive operations," just two days after they had set sail from England. Another surprise was in store for Eric and Florence, one much closer to home. Just as they were about to dock, they noticed a rash on both of their daughters. Patricia and Heather had come down with German measles, a highly contagious childhood disease. When no hotel rooms could be found for the family with their sick little girls, the Liddells returned to the deserted ship, only to find that their bedding had already been stripped.

Eric and Florence considered their situation as night fell on the empty vessel. They had been spared from the torpedo and spared an even more aggressive attack from a world power. More than ever before, Eric and Florence were convinced that God had preserved them and their daughters so that they could return to China.

They would go only where He led, and only with His strength, wisdom, and courage.

Tientsin in October 1940 was not the city they remembered. Japan had honored its alliance with Germany by positioning a military force outside the French enclave, a force that was openly hostile to all Westerners. Still, the enclave would have to be Florence and the two girls' home as long as the London Missionary Society maintained a presence there. And they would be there as long as Eric was in Siaochang.

As Eric neared the compound at Siaochang, he gasped in shock. The Japanese had erected a new wall around the village, one that resembled a garrison, or as Eric liked to say, "one of the outposts of the Empire." The peasants who had once called Siaochang home were now treated like members of a chain gang, forced to go out each day and destroy their own fields and graveyards to build roads for the enemy.

Inside the mission hospital, the situation had become equally dire. Whenever a nearby village was systematically destroyed, the casualties of war filled every bed and spilled out into the corridors of the rather primitive facility. Missionaries were kept busy night and day sterilizing instruments and changing dressings—and then enduring yet another official Japanese inspection. Food to feed the many refugees was running out, and despite pleas from the missionaries, the local Chinese leaders refused to give any help.

"We beg for food for our refugees, but they give neither grain nor a stove to boil grain," one missionary complained to Eric. "They have seen us caring for hundreds of their own people. We have cared for hundreds, and the mind cannot face the thought of what happened to the many hundreds more who could not come to us."

Meanwhile, Eric continued his itinerant preaching with his translator Wang. As he wrote to a family member, "When I am out it is giving, giving, all the time, and trying to get to know the people, and trying to leave them a message of encouragement and peace in a time when there is no external peace at all."

Before entering any village, Eric always noticed an older man sitting near the gate. This man was there to identify any danger to the village and to report it in a secret manner. Eric and Wang were allowed to enter most areas, including some villages to the southwest of Siaochang to which Eric had never gone. At one, he even performed a wedding to the ever-present sounds of gunfire in the distance. The guests were silent throughout the service, even though Eric could detect the love and joy in the newly married couple.

As Eric and Wang returned to Siaochang, however, they were mistaken for part of the Eighth Route Army. Scrambling off their bikes, they headed for any shelter they could find. Several rounds were fired at them, missing the two men. Finally, the Japanese soldiers realized their mistake and stopped their pursuit. Eric and Wang reached the compound safely.

But time was running out for the missionaries, and by Christmas 1940, rumors were rife that very soon all Westerners would be forced to leave China or perhaps be interned in prison camps. Annie, for one, didn't want to go back to Scotland, not while she still felt she was needed in China. Sensing Eric shared her feelings, she confided in him her plans.

"I've decided to ask the Japanese officials for a

transfer," she announced one evening as they were cleaning up at the hospital.

"But you know they won't want to grant that, Annie. The Japanese want us out of here, permanently. That's obvious, isn't it? Their constant attacks, their made-up inspections, the drunken soldiers everywhere." Eric looked deeply concerned. "Besides, where would you go?"

Annie looked him straight in the eye. "To Peking, to the Union Memorial Hospital. Yes, I've already thought it through. I know it's not safe to stay on the Great Plain anymore, but I just can't leave. In a bigger hospital, the needs will be great as the war continues. And I can't see it ending anytime soon, especially with the United States not committed yet."

Eric threw her a skeptical look, but he didn't doubt that she was up to the challenge. A month later, after enduring Annie's persistent pleas, the Japanese office allowed the petite, feisty Scotswoman to go to Peking—with the stipulation that she could not return to Siaochang.

Two months later, in February 1941, the Japanese made sure that no one would return to Siaochang ever again. The missionaries were given two weeks to pack their belongings and leave the compound, by order of the Japanese government. When two weeks passed, they were then told they could take nothing with them—just the clothes on their backs.

As Eric and the others walked out of the village gates on the dusty road to the railway station that would take them to Tientsin, he looked back at the garrisoned compound. In his head he could hear the voices of the country people he loved—"Ask Li Mu Shi," they said almost daily, or "Li Mu Shi will settle it." In his heart he knew he would never see them or Siaochang again.

A few weeks later, word spread to Tientsin that the Japanese had destroyed every beam and brick of Siaochang, leaving only rubble.

Years later, Annie would remember asking Eric if he had any regrets about coming back to Siaochang, despite the horrendous conditions and constant threat of war. "Never," Eric said, the dimple in his chin more pronounced than ever in his gaunt face. "I have never had so much joy!"

Eric returned to Tientsin, glad to be together with his family but sad about the situation in Siaochang. He knew, however, that he and Florence would not be together long. In March, the rumors that all British and American citizens living in China would be interned in special camps gained credence. After discussions with the London Missionary Society board, Eric and his sponsors reached a joint decision: Florence and the girls should return to Canada while it was still possible.

The deciding vote had been cast, figuratively,

by the one not yet present. Florence had discovered she was pregnant, and the baby would arrive in September. Neither Eric nor the board could predict what might be happening then, but all signs pointed to a worsening of the present conflict.

In May, after booking passage for his family on a ship bound for Canada, Eric said good-bye to Florence and his two daughters. Like other missionaries who had come to the port city of Kale to bid farewell to their wives and children, Eric hoped he would join them soon, but he still felt his place as a missionary was in China.

Kissing Florence's dark curls, Eric said softly, "Those who love God never meet for the last time." While Eric had never forgotten his mother's wise words, he didn't believe this would be his last time with Florence on this earth. *Like so many parting scenes of the past*, he thought, *this is just one more that will be erased in a few years' time.*

When Eric returned to Tientsin, he was invited to share an apartment in the French enclave with an old and treasured friend. A. P. Cullen, Eric's teacher and mentor at Eltham and his colleague at the Anglo-Chinese College, was only too happy to open his home to a now jobless missionary. For the next seven months, the two men would have plenty of time to plumb each other's thoughts and to take the long, rambling walks they both enjoyed. During the day, when A. P. went to the college, Eric busied himself writing letters to Florence, as well as continuing to work on a book he had started years before. Eric envisioned the slim volume, which he had titled *Manual of Christian Discipleship*, to be a guidebook for Chinese pastors.

The manual contained sixty pages of Bible readings, with comments for every day of the year, but it also divulged several keys to the man who was Eric Liddell. One page was devoted to a routine he had maintained for years, that of his "daily morning quiet." Every morning he would ask himself these questions:

1. Have I surrendered this new day to God, and will I seek and obey the guidance of the Holy Spirit throughout its hours?
2. What have I specially to thank God for this morning?
3. Is there any sin in my life for which I should seek Christ's forgiveness and cleansing? Is there any apology or restitution to make?
4. For whom does God want me to pray this morning?
5. What bearing does this morning's Bible passage have on my life, and what does He want me to do about it?
6. What does God want me to do today and how does He want me to do it?

Eric had continued to praise God for the answers to those questions in Edinburgh, Tientsin, and most especially, Siaochang. In September, he received another reason to thank God. Florence cabled the news of the birth of their third daughter, whom she had named Maureen.

"Wonderful news. Love, Eric" was his tersely worded reply that could not begin to convey his true feelings. He couldn't wait for the war to be over so he could hold his new baby daughter. He couldn't wait to feel truly useful again.

But the war was far from over. Japan's aggressive attack on Pearl Harbor in December produced repercussions in the occupied areas of China. Pearl Harbor would mean the end of life as Eric had known it. . .and the beginning of his final race for the prize.

THIRTEEN

From Tientsin to Weihsien, 1941–43

Within a few weeks of the attack on Pearl Harbor, Eric had been forced out of his home and his church. Once again, he struggled to stay busy, despite such upheavals.

When all London Missionary Society missionaries were forced to evacuate the French enclave, Eric was only too glad to accept the hospitality of the Reverend Howard Smith, a Methodist missionary in the English concession. Reverend Smith lived in a spacious home similar to the one the Liddells once occupied, complete with a tennis court as well as a lawn for cricket. Since the athlete in Eric was never far from the surface, he reveled in teaching Reverend Smith's daughters the fundamentals of tennis and in organizing impromptu cricket exhibitions among the

Methodist staff. To earn his keep since he had no income, Eric helped with household chores.

At the same time, the Anglo-Chinese College had been closed, as well as all churches. No Westerner was allowed to hold church services or to congregate in assemblies of more than ten people. Moreover, all foreigners were forced to wear armbands, declaring the country of their citizenship. When food became rationed in the English concession, Eric gladly volunteered to stand in the early morning bread lines before his "daily morning quiet." But his daily rounds were confined to a rather small area, as no Westerner living in the English concession was allowed to leave its boundaries.

Eric could abide by those regulations, for the most part, but he would not be denied a time of Sunday worship. And God blessed him with an idea that was destined to succeed.

"Every Sunday, we'll invite different groups of friends to meet at different homes for tea parties," Eric proposed to Howard Smith. "If we keep the number of guests to under ten, who will be the wiser?"

Reverend Smith nodded slowly. "But who will give the sermon?"

"I've already considered that, old chap. When the hostess passes out the tea cakes, she'll also hand out papers with the sermon printed on them, and all parties will receive the same sermon. Shall we give it a go?"

After an uneventful trial run, the Sunday tea parties became a fixture in the English concession. Because the Japanese never suspected what was really going on at these Sunday socials, the practice continued.

While Eric continued writing long—and censored—letters to his family, most of the Western world received little news of the missionaries trapped in China. What information was available was contained in the magazines published by the London Missionary Society and the China Inland Mission. Some excerpts from *China's Millions,* published by the China Inland Mission, are especially insightful:

> *We must remind our friends that we are no longer allowed to transmit personal gifts to missionaries in China as in prewar days. . . .*
>
> *At the present moment no British women are allowed to sail for "occupied" China, and we have to suspend, just for the moment, the training of women recruits. . . .*
>
> *One of the senior Japanese officers in Kaifeng. . .has been very friendly during the last few weeks as a result of [a missionary doctor] having located, by means of the hospital X-ray machine, a bullet which had lodged in his chest. . . .*
>
> *The Japanese erected electrified barricades around the British concession in Tientsin, stationing sentries and police at the various entrances and exits. . . .*

The Generalissimo [Chiang Kai-shek], speaking in Chunking to a missionary group, said: "We still need and welcome Christians from other lands who will serve the people. Do not feel that you are guests. You are comrades working with us to serve and save our people and to build a new nation."

All news would cease within a year as the Japanese stepped up their plans to intern Westerners remaining in China. By August 1942, forms were sent to all "enemy nationals," as the Japanese referred to the Westerners, requiring them to indicate whether they wanted to stay or leave the country. Most missionaries indicated their preference to stay, preferring to wait out the war. At the time, Eric had been offered a rural pastorate in western Canada, and he wrote Flo excitedly about the prospect. But he was thinking of taking the position after the war, not while China was still in such turmoil.

By early 1943, still no action had been taken toward the missionaries or any other Westerners. Eric expected something to happen very soon. Something *had* to happen soon. They couldn't remain in this unsettled state much longer.

At noon on March 12, 1943, the edict was delivered: All British and American enemy nationals living in Tientsin were to report to an internment camp in Weihsien. To avoid the connotation of prison camps and prisoners, the Japanese preferred to call the camp at Weihsien a "Civil Assembly Center" and those who resided there "civil internees."

In three parties on three consecutive days, the Westerners from Tientsin, Peking, and Tsingtao would leave for Weihsien, located in Shantung Province. Eric, who was appointed captain of his party, would leave on March 30. He had received very specific orders. All internees would be allowed to send four pieces of luggage ahead of time—by March 26—and to carry two suitcases with them.

They would need bedding as well as clothes for all kinds of weather. But what they would need most was likely forgotten in the shuffle. Few had remembered to pack dishes, and fewer still had brought knives, forks, and spoons.

For the second time in Eric's life, his departure from a city would be the occasion for a monumental spectacle. The first time, when he left Edinburgh for China, was marked by sincere devotion and support. The second would be a cruel travesty of the first.

On the day of Eric's departure, Japanese soldiers met his group at an appointed location in the English concession. All luggage was searched by the soldiers. Then they were led out of the concession, all of them carrying their own suitcases, children included, for the long walk to the train station.

The route had been carefully chosen by the enemy, and Chinese residents had been lined up hours ahead of time to witness the Westerners' departure. But instead of cheering or crying or showing any emotion, the Chinese, ever fearful of repercussions, stood stone-faced, watching the parade, some waving their hands weakly. Many of the missionaries struggled with their suitcases, tripping over their feet, or needing to stop for a rest. They were pushed on by the soldiers, on toward the train that would finally carry them away.

By midnight the filthy train was packed, with every seat taken. As captain, Eric was among the very last to find a seat. Squeezing his body into the tight surroundings, he removed several layers of clothing that would not fit into his suitcases and found his small, tattered Bible. He had carried it with him so it wouldn't be confiscated by the Japanese. Besides, he knew he wouldn't sleep much that night. He would need to be in God's Word.

Turning to a page he had marked earlier, he shared with another passenger Paul's words to Timothy: "Thou therefore endure hardness, as a good soldier of Jesus Christ. No man that warreth entangleth himself with the affairs of this life; that he may please him who hath chosen him to be a soldier. And if a man also strive for masteries, yet is he not crowned, except he strive lawfully" (2 Timothy 2:3–5).

"We are now truly soldiers for Jesus!" Eric exclaimed to no one in particular. And with that thought, the train began its laborious journey. They would change trains in Tainan in the morning, and arrive at Weihsien late the following afternoon.

FOURTEEN

Weihsien, 1943–44

The characters on the sign could be translated "The Courtyard of the Happy Way," but no internee arriving at the end of March would have described the camp in such glowing terms. Even in the dusk of early evening, the gray-brick, institutional-looking buildings surrounded by a forbidding barbed wire fence, which Eric and his group first spied from a distance, hardly seemed cheerful. But the worst was yet to come.

Located two miles from the city of Weihsien, the camp was housed in the former quarters of an American Presbyterian mission station, a station that had served a purpose similar to the compound at Siaochang. As in Siaochang, the Japanese had seized control of the station shortly after the attack on Pearl

Harbor, evicting all the missionaries.

But because this was an American mission, the soldiers' reaction upon entering had been far from orderly. The acclaimed victory at Pearl Harbor had incited the soldiers to a moblike mentality, and they acted on their feelings by trashing the inside of the mission. Not a dish was left intact; not a piece of furniture was still functional. There were no cooking utensils to be found, except a few mangled ones scattered in the debris.

The entire compound measured 150 by 200 yards, which would prove extremely tight quarters for the eighteen hundred internees, more than half of whom were children. (Six months later, some 250 more retired missionaries, staff, and children of missionaries from the Chefoo school, which Jenny Liddell had attended, would add to the camp's population.) As at Siaochang, there was a hospital, school, chapel, and living facilities, as well as a large meeting hall and kitchen with three ovens. Married couples with children would find themselves in rooms measuring no more than thirteen by nine feet, and unmarried males and females were grouped according to gender in similarly confined areas. The first night, as Eric helped his group find their rooms, the wails of young children rang out from all directions. For the first five months, he would share a room with two missionary pastors.

Because the war had severely crippled Japan's

military reserves, the internees were given few rules, little supervision, and minimal rations. The camp commander was a civil servant who supervised a staff of former policemen, not military officers. Clearly, the Japanese were not worried that a group made up primarily of missionaries would mount a daring escape. Still, there were terrifying reminders of the formidable enemy that was Japan: Electric fences surrounded the camp, and powerful searchlights circled the area continually through the night. Mandatory roll call was held twice every day.

All prisoners were assigned jobs, and by the time Eric arrived, the system was already in place. Because his group had been the last to arrive, the internees from Peking and Tsingtao were already working, with most of them helping in the kitchen. Some ladled out the portions, while others washed the dirty dishes. Many were professionals—bankers, importers, and professors—who had never done such tasks, at least not in recent memory.

After his first full day, Eric felt numbed by the mealtime routine. All internees would stand in a line, bowl and spoon in hand, to receive a thin broth and bread. Surveying the line, Eric exclaimed to Howard Smith, "Why, the line's got to be at least seventy yards long! Somehow we will have to make this camp a better place."

Howard knew only too well that Eric meant what he said. "But it will be hard to bring about change when all you're thinking about is how hungry you are!"

Within weeks, the camp would become a remarkably civilized community, due to the efforts of many internees. Committees were formed to supervise discipline, education, finance, quarters and accommodations, supplies, and athletics. An employment committee made sure that all able-bodied internees worked three hours every day, while an engineering and repairs committee organized a campaign to rebuild the damaged interiors. Entertainment programs were scheduled by the internees themselves, with performances of Handel's *Messiah* and George Bernard Shaw's *Androcles and the Lion* receiving rave reviews.

For his part, Eric took on more responsibilities than anyone could reasonably handle. Unlike the Chinese, who had no idea he was an Olympic champion, most Westerners had recognized him upon his arrival at the camp. At first, he was the camp's foremost celebrity, the one greeted by sidelong looks and whispers. But very soon, he was a friend to all. Known as "Uncle Eric," he became the children's math and science teacher, coach and teacher of all sports, minister of chapel services, warden of two dormitories, and translator for the Japanese.

Despite the ever-present hunger, Eric managed to generate enthusiasm for all kinds of sports, and he delighted in rounding up teams for various competitions. He would often be seen using Florence's old curtains and tablecloths, not to mention dresses and shirts, to mend hockey sticks and old baseballs just so the games could go on.

He also supervised two large buildings which housed more than two hundred single men and women. Every morning and evening, he had to make sure that all were present for the camp's roll calls; every day, he was involved in the more mundane tasks of fetching water and coal, emptying garbage, and cleaning various rooms. In the evening, he spent time tutoring those who needed extra help with their studies, especially in science and math.

As the leader of what was dubbed the Weihsien Christian Fellowship, Eric conducted Bible studies and served as a Christian counselor as well. With his permanent smile and easygoing manner, he was seen as the person to turn to, as one internee would say, "When personal relationships got just too impossible. . .he had a gentle, humorous way of soothing ruffled tempers and bringing to one's mind some bygone happiness or the prospect of some future interest round the corner 'when we got out.'"

His newly discovered talent for counseling would become invaluable in the months to come as he became more involved with the large population of young men and women. Teenagers at the camp, who felt confined and restless, were drawn to Eric because of his active nature and love of sports. But very soon, they presented a daunting challenge to him, one he never dreamed he would face. They wanted to hold hockey games on Sundays.

"You know I can't go along with that," Eric said when they first asked. "I have never gone against that principle, and I won't start now."

A group of them had gathered around him, and their groans and protests filled his ears. "You don't have to be there, Uncle Eric," one boy said. "We'll hold it ourselves, boys against girls. It'll be great!"

Eric could not stop them from going ahead with their plan, but he didn't have to tell them that he wouldn't be there to referee. And what he expected to happen did: The hockey game turned into a free-for-all, with tempers flaring and accusations flying. The next Sunday, when the teenagers decided to try again, they couldn't believe their eyes. Walking across the crude playing field to meet them was Eric.

"This Sunday, we'll play by the rules, for a change," he said rather sternly, and then, like the sun appearing from behind dark clouds, his usual big smile transformed his features. He had broken his rule for the greater good of the needs of his young friends.

Eric became a favorite speaker at the camp's church services, conducted without constraint from the Japanese captors. There was no need for Sunday tea parties at Weihsien and no limit on how many could attend the variety of services. Music was an integral part of the day, with a Salvation Army band playing hymns in an open square in the morning and a hymn sing taking place on Sunday evenings.

Eric's two favorite sermon topics were Paul's "love letter" to the Corinthians (1 Corinthians 13) and Jesus' Sermon on the Mount (Matthew 5–7). When asked why he went back to these passages time and again, Eric said, "These words are the cornerstone of my faith. . .this is the way love can be translated into living."

Years earlier, before he had left for Siaochang, Eric had written a little booklet called *The Sermon on the Mount: For Sunday School Teachers*. Writing about meekness and weakness, he stated the following:

> *What is the difference? Both may be kind and gentle. Is the difference the element of fear?*
> *Meek—kind and gentle and fearless.*
> *Weak—kind and gentle and led by fear.*
> *Meek—is love in the presence of wrong.*

Every morning this meek man still crawled out of bed at six and sat at his small table, his Bible and notebook open. Sometimes one of his roommates would join him, intrigued by this man who was so many things to so many people. After reading and praying, Eric would write in his notebook what needed to be done that day. In whatever circumstances he found himself, he knew first and foremost that his life was grounded in God, and that he would find the strength to show love in the presence of his enemies—and in the presence of his friends.

Annie Buchan was not supposed to be sent to Weihsien in the first place. She had been taking care of a very ill patient at the British Consulate in Peking, assured that she was exempt from internment because of her humane treatment of others. But that was before two internees managed to escape from Weihsien—the only two who would ever do so—and before the Japanese decided to exact reprisal for their actions. Annie had not seen Eric for years, not since their final day together at Siaochang.

But now, several months after Eric had arrived at Weihsien, Annie also came to the camp. She spotted him striding toward her, unaware of her presence. At first, she wasn't sure it was he, so changed was his appearance. His shirt had been made from some wildly colorful fabric, and he had lost most of his hair. He was also much thinner, and his skin had the burnished look of one who spends much time outdoors.

But she could never mistake his smile, once he recognized her, and his wild, infectious laugh. "Can you guess where I got this shirt?" he asked her in greeting.

Annie laughed and smiled back at him. "Did Florence give it to you?"

"In a way, yes, she did, but I doubt she'd like to see it on my back!" After a few minutes of cajoling,

Eric revealed the source: Florence's living-room curtains in Tientsin. *Only Eric could stride blithely around an internment camp wearing something as garish as that,* Annie thought. "Oh, Eric, I am so glad to see you!" she exclaimed suddenly, grabbing his arm.

In the months that followed, Annie would see her friend from time to time, whenever he would visit patients at the hospital. One of her biggest surprises was the quality of care at the hospital, despite the dearth of medical equipment and supplies. There were so many medical missionaries at the camp—doctors and nurses—that during more than two years of internment not a single internee died from any bacterial epidemic.

Still, Annie wondered, as well as everyone else at Weihsien, when the war would end. Since April, they had received an English language newspaper, but one that was highly censored. Eric and Annie joked about how the Japanese could possibly be winning every single battle against a host of formidable adversaries.

One day, as Eric was returning from another session of translating for the Weihsien Civil Affairs officer, he made a special trip to the hospital. After twelve years in China, in both urban and rural communities, Eric's Chinese was considered fluent.

"They're blocking out entire battles in that newspaper," he said when he found Annie. "The tide is turning in the war; I'm sure of it now, and the

Allies are finally in a good position. Besides that, the Japanese are truly fighting a losing battle here in China. Maybe I'll be able to see Flo and the girls sooner than I thought."

Although the alliance between Mao Tse-tung and Chiang Kai-shek was unraveling, the Communist and Nationalist forces were too great in China's hinterland for the Japanese to gain a foothold. Since 1941, the Communists had been fighting both the Nationalists and the Japanese, and the Nationalists were also waging war on several fronts. To aid her husband's cause, Madame Chiang Kai-shek made a tour of the United States and Great Britain with the stated purpose of enlisting support for her husband's regime and help in expelling the Japanese from China. But her speeches were designed to stir up sentiments against the Communists and Mao Tse-tung, as well. And bearing in mind the composition of her audiences, she spoke very flatteringly of the American and British missionaries imprisoned in China. As the war continued taking its toll on Japanese forces, Western pressure came to bear on the situation in the internment camps. But whatever improvements Eric noticed were only temporary.

For a time, the internees were offered Chinese products for sale at a canteen on the camp's premises, and for a price one could supplement the camp diet with peanuts, eggs, candy, and fruit. Internees were also allowed to receive Red Cross messages from home on special letter forms, but these tersely worded greetings were limited to one hundred words. After a while, the limit was reduced by the Japanese to twenty-five words.

The news from home for Eric was far from cheerful. His brother Ernest, a lieutenant in the Royal Artillery, suffered a severe cranial injury in battle and was sent home to recuperate. While Eric was spared many details, he discovered that his mother was terminally ill and that his imprisonment had been kept from her. They had not parted for the last time, Eric consoled himself, remembering again her last words to him.

On the other side of the Atlantic, the news from Canada was always upbeat and filled with the achievements of three little girls. Although Eric never went anywhere without carrying pictures of his family in his pocket, he only showed them to his closest friends. He was not one to share his burdens with others, figuring that they were likely in the same position as he. Rather, as always, he sought to make the present better.

Since the arrival of those from the Chefoo school, Eric channeled his homesickness into the care of the children of other missionaries. He delighted in their education and athletic development, and many of them reminded him of his beloved Patricia and Heather, and of Maureen, whom he had seen only in photographs. In his heart he still felt certain he would see them again, he would hold their wiggly bodies, he would caress Flo's dark curls. The war was wearing down the Japanese. . . . It was only a matter of months.

As 1944 came to a close, Eric's optimism seemed justified. The war had indeed taken a turn for the worse for the Japanese, who needed to send most of their supplies to their fighting forces. Consequently, rations at Weihsien were cut alarmingly and the health of the internees was put at risk. (Japan's treatment of its military prisoners of war, many of whom starved to death, was even worse than its treatment of civilian prisoners.) Outbreaks of typhoid fever, malaria, and dysentery, as well as mental breakdowns, became common among the internees.

Even Eric, whose phenomenal strength and reserves of energy were an inspiration to many, began to show signs of the strain of eighteen months in captivity—but only to those who knew him best. Annie found him one day sitting on a bench in the open courtyard, his body bent over, the treasured photos of his family in his lap.

She quietly sat down next to him, her eyes cast in the distance. "What is it, Eric? Did you hear from Flo?" She could only assume that there was some problem with the girls.

Eric shook his head, then raised his tired body.

"No, thank God they're all fine. It's just. . .oh, Annie, I've started questioning myself. My big worry is that I didn't give Flo enough of my time." Tears had formed in his eyes, and on this occasion he let them fall down his cheeks.

"But, Eric, even you say the war should be ending soon. You'll be together with Flo and the girls before you know it." Annie's words could not erase the furrows in his brow. "There's something else you're not telling me, isn't there?"

Eric turned away from her for a moment. "I don't know how to say this. . .perhaps I feel the way I do about Flo. . ." He couldn't continue for a moment, and then he cleared his throat. "It's just that I can't see any future for myself. Everything looks blank."

Annie watched as he made his way back to his dormitory, his clothes hanging loosely on his shrunken frame, his gait slow and deliberate, his head hung down. *It isn't like him to walk like that,* Annie thought, *and it isn't like him to have no hope.*

Christmas found the camp preparing for another pageant, which Eric participated in, but the season also brought losses. Eric spent many hours consoling the mother of a child who had been electrocuted by the high-powered fence that surrounded the camp. A. P. Cullen, Eric's longtime friend who was also at Weihsien, sent a card to Annie with this message: "God gave us a memory so that we might have roses in December."

To Eric, memory seemed a thing of the past. Though he spoke to no one about his deteriorating physical condition, he couldn't remember a time when he felt truly well. Perhaps his numbing headaches were a sign that he had been working too hard and just needed a bit of a rest. During his morning quiet on that late December morning, Eric flipped open his Bible and read the first verse that caught his eye: "I press toward the mark for the prize of the high calling of God in Christ Jesus" (Philippians 3:14).

FIFTEEN

Weihsien, 1945

The agonizing headaches would not go away, no matter what Eric did. By the middle of January they had become so debilitating, he decided to take a drastic step: He went to the hospital. When he saw Annie, his description of his problems hardly sounded like it was coming from the competent practitioner who had once assumed responsibility for the entire hospital at Siaochang.

"There's something seriously wrong inside my head," he told her.

While the doctors' diagnoses ranged from influenza to sinusitis to malnutrition, there appeared to be nothing wrong with him that was life-threatening, and Eric returned to his living quarters. Eric was malnourished, it was true, but so were most of the internees at Weihsien. At the end of the month, help had arrived in the form of basic foodstuff parcels sent by the International Red Cross. But food did not alleviate Eric's suffering.

Ever the vigilant nurse, Annie remained worried about him. Eric had been in ill health for some time, longer than he had wanted to admit to anyone. Ignoring camp rules, she barged into his room in the men's dormitory and then a short time later went directly to the head doctor at the hospital. Despite the lack of rooms, Annie found a way to have Eric admitted.

Eric was now showing the effects of a serious neurological condition. He spoke in a halting manner, one eye drooped, and he had great difficulty walking. In particular, his right leg was partially paralyzed. The doctors, though they certainly suspected a brain tumor, treated him for a stroke. There was nothing they could do for him in the facilities at Weihsien. Eric would remain at the hospital for three weeks, seeing few visitors and resting.

Annie now knew why he had given up hope a few months earlier and why the future had seemed blank to him. The tumor had affected his personality, and likely he was suffering from depression. While his faith remained intact, gone was his fun-loving nature.

Then, without explanation, Eric seemed to rally. For the first time in many weeks, he attended church services and even visited friends for tea.

On February 21, Eric went for a walk in the early afternoon on his way to the camp's post office. He had just written another tightly worded message to Flo, and despite the cold and overcast day, something beckoned him outdoors. In his rather jagged hand, he wrote her of his health concerns, while minimizing greatly the severity of his condition:

> *Was carrying too much responsibility. Slight nervous breakdown. Am much better after month in hospital. Doctor suggests changing my work. Giving up teaching and taking up physical work like baking. . .a good change. Keep me in touch with the news. Enjoying comfort and parcels. Special love to you and the children.*
>
> *Eric*

On his way to the post office, he met the wife of a former colleague at Tientsin who inquired whether he'd heard from Flo. Yes, he answered haltingly. Looking at him closely, she advised him, "You ought to be resting more, Eric."

Unwilling to discuss his condition in depth, Eric answered, "No, I must get my walking legs again." *There's no reason why I shouldn't be running again, refereeing hockey and rugby games. . .chasing after my girls. . .teaching them to use their arms to cross the finish line. Yes, Headmaster Hayward, once I did have apples in my cheeks, once long ago. Yes, Tom McKerchar, I still am a slow starter, but I know how to have a strong finish.*

Later in the afternoon, he proceeded back to the hospital, not for himself, but to visit patients in the wards. There he ran into a former Sunday school pupil from his days at Union Church in Tientsin. *Union Church. . .my father's church, and the church of my beloved. . .there's Flo at the organ. . .Flo laughing to meet me, when I couldn't remember her name. . .Flo walking down the aisle, with Jenny's veil trailing behind her, her hand clasping my trembling one.*

As he tried to talk, he started coughing and choking at the same time. Alarmed, his former pupil rushed down the hospital corridor to summon help. Annie, who was just going off her nursing shift, heard the commotion and quickly made her way to the room where Eric was lying on a bed. Seeing her, he smiled and whispered her name. *You will remember where we have been. . .Pei-tai-ho, Siaochang, and Weihsien. . .and you will tell others to come to China, with love in their hearts and the Word of God. Remember the miracles at Siaochang, how we were spared so many times, how the people were so hungry for the good news!*

"Eric, talk to me," said Annie urgently, her voice slicing through the fog of his mind. "What do you think is wrong?"

"They haven't a clue," he whispered back to her, a smile barely crinkling the corners of his mouth. *And*

I am the Knight of the Bath. . .laugh with me, Annie, and do not look so serious. . .do everything in love.

She sat with him, holding his hand for several minutes until she felt a tap on her shoulder. It was the duty physician, who told her she could go back to her dormitory since she had just finished a long shift. "No, I'll not leave him," she answered tersely.

Annie noticed Eric's breathing had become labored and he was fading in and out of consciousness, the symptoms of a cerebral hemorrhage. She had to find a doctor immediately. Running into the adjacent ward, she stopped two doctors who had treated Eric weeks earlier. "Do you realize Eric is dying?" she began, her voice rising in volume.

"Nonsense," they responded almost in unison. Annie turned her back on them and returned to the room where Eric was. She was just in time.

A few minutes later, Eric went into a convulsion, and Annie took him in her arms. Then he spoke to her for the last time. "Annie," he whispered, "it's complete surrender." Tears streaming down her face, she watched as he slipped into a coma, and then into the presence of God. The Olympic champion whose windmill style was a study in motion and whose love of God was known around the world was finally at rest.

Snow fell the next day, covering the camp like a clean white sheet and masking the despair evident in many faces. Shock had indeed greeted the news of Eric's death; very few had known how ill he was. Two days later, on February 24, the funeral was held at the large meeting hall at the camp, a room soon filled to capacity. Even on this bleak day, more stood outside than were allowed in during the service.

The Reverend Arnold Bryson, a longtime missionary associated with the London Missionary Society, spoke first of a man, only forty-three years old, taken in the prime of his life. But God does not make mistakes, he added, and this time was not the exception. Rather, Reverend Bryson chose to dwell on Eric's life and character and on the secret of his far-reaching influence.

"His was a God-controlled life and he followed his Master and Lord with devotion that never flagged and with an intensity of purpose that made men see both the reality and power of true religion. . . . Our friend, whose happy, radiant face. . .will surely live on in the hearts and lives of all who knew him."

Eight missionaries and friends carried Eric's plain coffin to the cemetery adjacent to the building where the Japanese officers lived. Oblivious to the biting winds and spitting snow, they marched, followed by an honor guard of Eric's students, the children from the Chefoo school. At the grave site, hundreds recited the Beatitudes, those verses that Eric had claimed for his own. "Blessed are the poor in spirit: for theirs is the kingdom of heaven. Blessed are they that mourn:

for they shall be comforted. Blessed are the meek: for they shall inherit the earth. . . . Blessed are the pure in heart: for they shall see God" (Matthew 5:3–5, 8).

Ten days later, the Weihsien mourners gathered again to be comforted at a memorial service for Eric, this time conducted by A. P. Cullen. A scrap of paper bearing Eric's handwriting had come to his attention, words written on the afternoon of Eric's final day. Apparently, at the hospital Eric had scribbled a message, and the words were especially telling. He had written the first line of a favorite hymn, "Be Still My Soul."

Staying in their seats, those gathered sang softly the words that Eric had cherished, written to the music of "Finlandia." A. P. Cullen would speak of his decades-long friendship, a former rugby teammate of Eric's shared his memories, and Annie spoke of their days at Siaochang, her diminutive frame barely visible behind the wooden lectern.

More than two months after Eric's death, Florence received visitors at her home in Toronto. Because of the war and the situation in the internment camps, the news of Eric's death had not yet reached her. Eric had, of course, written her of his health concerns, but she had no idea his condition was terminal until her visitors broke the sad news. She would receive three or four more letters from Eric after she learned of his death.

As the rest of the world began to assimilate the

news of Eric Liddell's death, other memorial services were held. The first was in Toronto, at Florence's church, to be followed by two services of note in Scotland. Morningside Congregational Church in Edinburgh, the church Eric had attended, accommodated more than a thousand mourners, including Rob, Jenny, and Ernest, as well as Eric's former headmaster, George Robertson, and D. P. Thomson. Then at the Dundas Street Congregational Church in Glasgow, the church where James Liddell had been ordained, saddened Scots again gathered, joined by D. P. and Rob. Concerned about the future of Florence and her daughters, D. P. formed a national committee to raise money for them and to commemorate the life of Eric Liddell.

In the months that followed Eric's death, a sense of lethargy descended over those at Weihsien. Gone was their smiling warrior, their tireless advocate, their spiritual conscience, their friend. Now they had only to wait out the war. Little did they know that the United States' bombing of Hiroshima and Nagasaki in early August would set the stage for the last days of fighting. In the middle of August, Annie was working in the hospital when she was startled by the sound of planes flying very close overhead. Suddenly, crashing through the windows, came cans of fruit juice.

In short order, United States paratroopers marched into camp, informed the Japanese officers that they had assumed command, and watched calmly as the Japanese evacuated Weihsien. Annie, along with the other British missionaries and civilians, was taken to Tsingtao and then to Hong Kong, before boarding a ship back to England. She would be home in Scotland by Christmas.

Even though Eric was not there to encourage her, she remembered a favorite scripture verse of his, one that his father had loved and that had inspired Eric at Tientsin and Siaochang. To the church at Corinth, Paul wrote, "Know ye not that they which run in a race run all, but one receiveth the prize? So run, that ye may obtain" (1 Corinthians 9:24).

Two years later, Annie Buchan returned to China.

In Memory of Eric Liddell
Tributes to the Olympic Runner
Who Ran the Good Race

Eric Liddell Challenge Trophy—Created in
1946, an award given to the best athlete
in track and field from more than 150
schools in Scotland.

Eric Liddell Memorial Room—Meeting
hall for Christian youth activities at
St. Ninian's Conference and Training
Centre, Edinburgh (since destroyed
by fire).

Liddell House—Boarding house (dormitory) at Eltham College, London.

Liddell Patrol—Third Hong Kong Sea
Scout Group (one of many Scout
patrols named for Eric Liddell).

Eric Liddell Boys' Club—Crieff, Scotland,
and in many other places.

Chariots of Fire—1981 film, produced
by David Puttnam and starring Ian
Charleson as Eric Liddell and Ben

Cross as Harold Abrahams, which garnered many awards, including the Academy Award for Best Picture.

Memorial Stone at Weihsien—Sponsored by Edinburgh University as a lasting tribute to one of its most famous alumni, the stone is placed near the site of Eric's grave. (The cemetery where he was buried was destroyed after the war.)

Eric Liddell Centre—A Christian community center in Edinburgh, funded by local churches and private donations, which provides specialized day care for the elderly, as well as counseling, exercise classes, and educational and community living courses for those with mental health problems.

Statue of Eric Liddell—Unveiled in 1998 by Eric's daughter, Mrs. Patricia Russell, the statue stands in the Old College of Edinburgh University.